" Bill Gates for President: A Vision

Written and Copyright by

2024©

Peter Cranberry Publishing

Albert Allen III

74478 HWY 111 Ste 175

Palm Desert, California. 92260

Email:officeofalbertallen@gmail.com

Registered Library of Congress.2024

Chapter 1: The Idea of Bill Gates as President

Background on Bill Gates

Bill Gates, born William Henry Gates III on October 28, 1955, in Seattle, Washington, is one of the most influential figures in the modern technological world. Raised in an upper-middle-class family, Gates showed an early interest in computer programming. His journey into the world of technology began in earnest during his high school years at Lakeside School, where he had access to a computer terminal and quickly became adept at programming.

In 1973, Gates enrolled at Harvard University, where he met Steve Ballmer, who would later become the CEO of Microsoft. However, Gates' passion for computer programming and the rapidly evolving tech industry led him to leave Harvard in 1975 to co-found Microsoft with his childhood friend, Paul Allen. This decision marked the beginning of a transformative era in technology and business.

Under Gates' leadership, Microsoft revolutionized the software industry by developing and popularizing the personal computer operating system, starting with MS-DOS and later, the Windows operating system. Gates' vision of "a computer on every desk and in every home" became a reality, and Microsoft grew to become one of the largest and most successful technology companies in the world.

Overview of His Accomplishments

Bill Gates' accomplishments extend far beyond the creation of Microsoft. His contributions to technology, business, and philanthropy have left an indelible mark on the world.

Microsoft and Technological Innovation:

Gates played a pivotal role in the development and commercialization of software that made personal computing accessible to millions.

Microsoft Windows became the dominant operating system for personal computers, setting industry standards and driving technological innovation.

Gates' leadership at Microsoft led to the creation of other essential software products, including Microsoft Office, which became a staple in business and education.

Philanthropy:

In 2000, Gates and his then-wife, Melinda, established the Bill & Melinda Gates Foundation, one of the largest private philanthropic foundations in the world.

The foundation focuses on global health, education, and poverty alleviation, investing billions of dollars in initiatives to combat diseases like malaria, HIV/AIDS, and tuberculosis.

Gates' commitment to philanthropy earned him recognition as one of the world's most generous and impactful philanthropists.

Thought Leadership:

Gates has authored several books, including "The Road Ahead" (1995), "Business @ the Speed of Thought" (1999), and "How to Avoid a Climate Disaster" (2021), sharing his insights on technology, business, and global challenges.

As a thought leader, Gates frequently speaks on issues such as climate change, global health, and education reform, advocating for innovative solutions to some of the world's most pressing problems.

Why He Would Consider Running for President

The idea of Bill Gates running for president may seem unconventional at first glance, but several factors make this a compelling proposition.

Visionary Leadership:

Gates' track record as a visionary leader who can anticipate and drive technological and societal changes positions him as a candidate capable of leading the nation into a future of innovation and progress.

His ability to think long-term and strategically would be invaluable in addressing complex national and global challenges.

Problem-Solving Expertise:

Gates has demonstrated exceptional problem-solving skills throughout his career, from developing groundbreaking software to tackling global health crises through his foundation.

His analytical and pragmatic approach to problem-solving could be instrumental in addressing issues such as economic inequality, healthcare reform, and climate change.

Philanthropic Impact:

Gates' extensive experience in philanthropy has given him a deep understanding of the interconnectedness of global issues and the importance of addressing root causes.

His commitment to improving lives through philanthropic initiatives reflects a genuine concern for the well-being of people, which would resonate with voters seeking a compassionate and effective leader.

Technological Expertise:

In an era where technology plays a crucial role in every aspect of society, Gates' expertise in technology and innovation would be a significant asset.

His insights into the digital economy, cybersecurity, and technological advancements would help shape policies that promote growth and protect national interests.

Global Perspective:

Gates' work on global health and development has given him a unique perspective on international relations and the interconnectedness of nations.

As president, he could leverage his global network and experience to foster international cooperation and address global challenges collaboratively.

Commitment to Education:

Gates' dedication to education reform and improving access to quality education aligns with the needs of a rapidly changing workforce and society.

His focus on STEM (Science, Technology, Engineering, and Mathematics) education would prepare future generations for the challenges and opportunities of the digital age.

In conclusion, Bill Gates' extensive background, accomplishments, and unique skill set make the idea of his presidency both intriguing and viable. His visionary leadership, problem-solving expertise, philanthropic impact, technological prowess, global perspective, and commitment to education position him as a candidate capable of leading the United States into a prosperous and innovative future.

Chapter 2: Transformative Leadership

Gates' Leadership Style

Bill Gates' leadership style is characterized by a blend of visionary thinking, pragmatic problem-solving, and an unwavering commitment to innovation and excellence. Over the decades, Gates has honed a leadership approach that is both adaptable and forward-thinking, enabling him to navigate complex challenges and drive significant change. Here are some key aspects of his leadership style:

Visionary Thinking:

Future-Oriented: Gates has always been ahead of his time, envisioning a future where technology plays a central role in daily life. His foresight was evident in his early advocacy for personal computing and his current focus on artificial intelligence and clean energy.

Big Picture Focus: Gates is known for his ability to see the big picture and connect seemingly disparate dots. This holistic view allows him to identify trends and opportunities that others might overlook.

Pragmatic Problem-Solving:

Data-Driven Decisions: Gates relies heavily on data and empirical evidence to make decisions. He is known for his analytical approach, rigorously examining information before drawing conclusions.

Iterative Improvement: Rather than seeking perfection from the outset, Gates believes in continuous improvement. He advocates for the iterative process of developing, testing, and refining ideas and solutions.

Innovation and Excellence:

Encouraging Innovation: Gates fosters a culture of innovation, encouraging creative thinking and risk-taking. He understands that failure is a part of the innovation process and sees it as a learning opportunity.

High Standards: Gates sets high standards for himself and his team. His pursuit of excellence drives those around him to strive for the best possible outcomes.

Empathy and Humility:

Listening to Others: Gates values input from diverse perspectives and is known for his active listening skills. He believes that collaboration and open communication are key to effective leadership.

Acknowledging Limits: Despite his vast knowledge, Gates acknowledges his limitations and seeks advice from experts. This humility allows him to make well-informed decisions and build strong, knowledgeable teams.

Commitment to Social Impact:

Philanthropic Focus: Gates' leadership is deeply rooted in a commitment to social impact. His work through the Bill & Melinda Gates Foundation demonstrates his dedication to addressing global challenges and improving lives.

Ethical Leadership: Gates upholds high ethical standards in his professional and philanthropic endeavors, emphasizing the importance of integrity and responsibility.

How His Leadership Could Transform the Presidency

Bill Gates' unique leadership style has the potential to transform the presidency by introducing innovative approaches to governance, fostering collaboration, and driving forward-thinking policies. Here are several ways in which his leadership could bring about significant change:

Innovation-Driven Governance:

Technological Integration: Gates would likely prioritize the integration of advanced technologies into government operations, improving efficiency, transparency, and public access to services. This could include the use of AI, data analytics, and digital platforms to streamline processes and enhance decision-making.

R&D Investment: Gates' commitment to innovation would likely translate into increased investment in research and development across various sectors, including healthcare, energy, and education. This focus on R&D could spur economic growth and maintain the United States' competitive edge in global markets.

Evidence-Based Policy Making:

Data-Driven Decisions: Gates' data-driven approach would bring a new level of rigor to policy making. By relying on empirical evidence and scientific research, he could develop more effective and sustainable policies that address complex issues such as climate change, healthcare, and economic inequality.

Iterative Policy Development: Gates' iterative approach to problem-solving could lead to more adaptive and responsive policies. By continuously assessing and refining policies based on real-world outcomes, he could ensure that government actions are effective and aligned with evolving needs.

Collaborative Leadership:

Building Strong Teams: Gates' ability to build and lead diverse teams would be invaluable in government. By assembling experts from various fields and fostering a collaborative environment, he could tackle multifaceted challenges with comprehensive and innovative solutions.

Public-Private Partnerships: Gates' experience in both the private and philanthropic sectors positions him to effectively leverage public-private partnerships. These collaborations could drive progress in areas such as infrastructure, healthcare, and education, combining the strengths of different sectors for the public good.

Ethical and Transparent Governance:

High Ethical Standards: Gates' commitment to ethical leadership would set a strong example for government officials and help restore public trust in government institutions. By prioritizing integrity and accountability, he could foster a culture of transparency and responsibility.

Public Engagement: Gates' emphasis on listening to diverse perspectives would enhance public engagement in the political process. By actively seeking input from citizens and stakeholders, he could ensure that policies are inclusive and reflect the needs and aspirations of the broader population.

Long-Term Vision:

Strategic Planning: Gates' visionary thinking would bring a long-term perspective to governance. By focusing on future-oriented policies and strategic planning, he could address pressing issues such as climate change, technological disruption, and global health with foresight and proactive solutions.

Sustainable Development: Gates' commitment to sustainability would drive policies that balance economic growth with environmental protection and social equity. His leadership could promote sustainable development practices that benefit both current and future generations.

Education and Workforce Development:

Education Reform: Gates' dedication to improving education would likely result in significant reforms aimed at enhancing the quality and accessibility of education. By promoting STEM education and lifelong learning, he could prepare the workforce for the demands of the digital economy.

Skill Development: Gates' focus on skill development would help bridge the gap between education and employment, ensuring that individuals have the skills needed to thrive in a rapidly changing job market.

Global Leadership:

International Cooperation: Gates' global perspective and network of international connections would enhance the United States' role in global affairs. By fostering international cooperation on issues such as climate change, global health, and technology regulation, he could strengthen the country's leadership on the world stage.

Global Health Initiatives: Gates' experience in global health could inform policies that address pandemics and other health crises more effectively. By prioritizing global health security, he could help prevent and mitigate future health emergencies.

In conclusion, Bill Gates' transformative leadership style, characterized by visionary thinking, pragmatic problem-solving, innovation, empathy, and a commitment to social impact, has the potential to revolutionize the presidency. His approach to governance could drive technological integration, evidence-based policy making, collaborative leadership, ethical governance, long-term vision, education reform, and global leadership, positioning the United States for a prosperous and sustainable future.

Chapter 3: Vision for America

Gates' Vision for the Future of America

Bill Gates envisions an America that is prosperous, innovative, equitable, and sustainable. His vision encompasses a holistic approach to national development, emphasizing technological advancement, economic growth, social equity, and environmental sustainability. Gates believes in leveraging technology and innovation to solve pressing challenges, fostering a dynamic and inclusive economy, and ensuring a high quality of life for all citizens.

A Technologically Advanced Society:

Gates foresees a future where advanced technologies are seamlessly integrated into everyday life, enhancing productivity, connectivity, and quality of life. He envisions widespread adoption of artificial intelligence, quantum computing, and other cutting-edge technologies to drive economic and social progress.

A Thriving Economy:

Gates envisions an economy that is robust, resilient, and inclusive. He aims to create a dynamic economic environment that fosters entrepreneurship, innovation, and sustainable growth, ensuring that the benefits of economic prosperity are broadly shared.

An Equitable Society:

Gates is committed to addressing social inequities and ensuring that all Americans have access to opportunities and resources necessary for a fulfilling life. He envisions a society where disparities in education, healthcare, and economic opportunity are significantly reduced.

A Sustainable Future:

Gates envisions a future where environmental sustainability is a core principle of national development. He aims to address climate change, promote renewable energy, and ensure the responsible use of natural resources to protect the planet for future generations.

His Plans for Economic Growth, Technology, and Innovation

Bill Gates' plans for economic growth, technology, and innovation are rooted in his deep understanding of these areas and his commitment to leveraging them for the greater good. Here are some key components of his vision and plans:

Driving Economic Growth:

Support for Small and Medium-Sized Enterprises (SMEs): Gates recognizes the critical role that SMEs play in the economy. He plans to implement policies that provide access to capital, reduce regulatory burdens, and offer technical assistance to help these businesses thrive.

Infrastructure Investment: Gates believes in the importance of modern infrastructure for economic growth. He plans to invest in upgrading transportation, communication, and energy infrastructure to support business development and improve quality of life.

Inclusive Economic Policies: Gates aims to implement policies that promote economic inclusivity, ensuring that marginalized communities have access to economic opportunities. This includes targeted investments in education, job training, and entrepreneurship programs.

Advancing Technology and Innovation:

Research and Development (R&D): Gates plans to increase investment in R&D to drive technological innovation. He envisions public-private partnerships that leverage government funding and private sector expertise to advance scientific research and technological development.

Digital Infrastructure: Gates aims to expand and modernize digital infrastructure to support the widespread adoption of emerging technologies. This includes ensuring high-speed internet access for all Americans and developing secure, reliable digital networks.

Innovation Hubs: Gates plans to establish innovation hubs across the country to foster collaboration between academia, industry, and government. These hubs will serve as centers of excellence for research, development, and commercialization of new technologies.

Promoting Education and Workforce Development:

STEM Education: Gates is a strong advocate for STEM (Science, Technology, Engineering, and Mathematics) education. He plans to enhance STEM curricula in schools, provide scholarships for STEM students, and promote STEM careers to prepare the workforce for the demands of the digital economy.

Lifelong Learning: Gates recognizes the importance of continuous learning in a rapidly changing job market. He plans to support initiatives that provide access to ongoing education and skill development, enabling workers to adapt to new technologies and job opportunities.

Equity in Education: Gates aims to address disparities in education by ensuring that all students have access to high-quality educational resources and opportunities. This includes investing in underfunded schools, providing teacher training, and supporting programs that promote educational equity.

Addressing Climate Change and Promoting Sustainability:

Renewable Energy: Gates is committed to transitioning to a clean energy economy. He plans to invest in renewable energy sources such as solar, wind, and hydroelectric power, and to promote energy efficiency in homes, businesses, and transportation.

Carbon Reduction: Gates aims to implement policies that reduce carbon emissions, including carbon pricing, stricter emissions standards, and support for carbon capture and storage technologies.

Sustainable Agriculture: Gates plans to promote sustainable agricultural practices that protect the environment and ensure food security. This includes supporting research on climate-resilient crops, reducing food waste, and promoting regenerative farming practices.

Fostering Innovation in Healthcare:

Healthcare Access: Gates envisions a healthcare system where all Americans have access to affordable, high-quality healthcare. He plans to support initiatives that expand healthcare coverage, reduce costs, and improve the quality of care.

Medical Research: Gates aims to increase funding for medical research to develop new treatments and cures for diseases. He envisions public-private partnerships that accelerate the translation of scientific discoveries into practical healthcare solutions.

Global Health Initiatives: Gates plans to continue his work in global health, focusing on initiatives that address infectious diseases, maternal and child health, and health system strengthening in developing countries.

Building a Resilient Society:

Disaster Preparedness: Gates plans to enhance national preparedness for natural disasters, pandemics, and other emergencies. This includes investing in early warning systems, strengthening public health infrastructure, and promoting community resilience.

Cybersecurity: Gates recognizes the growing threat of cyberattacks and plans to implement robust cybersecurity measures to protect critical infrastructure, businesses, and individuals from cyber threats.

Social Safety Nets: Gates aims to strengthen social safety nets to support individuals and families facing economic hardship. This includes expanding access to unemployment benefits, housing assistance, and food security programs.

In my summary, Bill Gates' vision for America encompasses a comprehensive approach to national development, emphasizing technological advancement, economic growth, social equity, and environmental sustainability. His plans for economic growth, technology, and innovation are designed to create a prosperous and inclusive society, where all Americans have the opportunity to thrive in a rapidly changing world. Through strategic investments in infrastructure, education, healthcare, and sustainability, Gates aims to build a resilient and dynamic nation poised for success in the 21st century.

Chapter 4: The Microsoft Era

Founding and Growing Microsoft

The story of Microsoft begins in 1975 when Bill Gates and his childhood friend Paul Allen co-founded the company. Their journey from a small startup to a global tech giant is a tale of vision, innovation, perseverance, and strategic acumen.

The Early Days:

Inspiration and Formation: Bill Gates and Paul Allen were inspired by the release of the Altair 8800, a microcomputer kit developed by MITS (Micro Instrumentation and Telemetry Systems). They saw an opportunity to develop software for this new computer. In 1975, they wrote a version of the BASIC programming language for the Altair, which marked the beginning of Microsoft (originally spelled Micro-Soft, short for microcomputer software).

Partnership with MITS: The success of their BASIC interpreter for the Altair led to a contract with MITS, providing the young company with its first significant revenue stream. This partnership helped Microsoft gain a foothold in the nascent personal computer industry.

Early Challenges and Breakthroughs:

Initial Struggles: In the early years, Microsoft faced numerous challenges, including limited financial resources and intense competition from established companies. However, Gates and Allen's determination and belief in their vision kept them moving forward.

IBM Partnership: A major breakthrough came in 1980 when IBM approached Microsoft to provide an operating system for its first personal computer, the IBM PC. Microsoft acquired an existing operating system called QDOS (Quick and Dirty Operating System), refined it, and licensed it to IBM as MS-DOS. This partnership was a turning point for Microsoft, significantly boosting its credibility and market presence.

The Rise of Windows:

Development of Windows: Recognizing the limitations of MS-DOS and the potential of graphical user interfaces (GUIs), Microsoft began developing Windows, an operating system with a GUI. The first version, Windows 1.0, was released in 1985. While it received a lukewarm reception, it laid the groundwork for future iterations.

Windows 3.0 and Market Dominance: The release of Windows 3.0 in 1990 marked a significant milestone. With its improved interface and enhanced capabilities, it became a commercial success, establishing Windows as the dominant operating system for personal computers. Subsequent versions, including Windows 95 and Windows XP, cemented Microsoft's position as a leader in the software industry.

Expansion and Diversification:

Office Suite: In addition to Windows, Microsoft developed a suite of productivity applications known as Microsoft Office. The initial release included Word, Excel, and PowerPoint, which became essential tools for businesses and individuals worldwide.

Internet Explorer and the Internet Era: During the 1990s, Microsoft recognized the growing importance of the internet. The company launched Internet Explorer, its web browser, which played a crucial role in the early days of web browsing and became the most widely used browser for many years.

Gaming and Entertainment: Microsoft also ventured into the gaming industry with the launch of the Xbox console in 2001. This move diversified Microsoft's product portfolio and established it as a significant player in the gaming market.

Navigating Challenges:

Antitrust Litigation: As Microsoft grew, it faced legal challenges, most notably the antitrust case brought by the U.S. Department of Justice in the late 1990s. The case centered on allegations that Microsoft had used its market dominance to stifle competition. The company reached a settlement in 2001, agreeing to certain conduct restrictions while continuing to innovate and grow.

Adapting to Technological Shifts: The rise of the internet and mobile computing presented new challenges and opportunities. Microsoft adapted by shifting its focus to cloud computing with the launch of Azure, its cloud platform, and by acquiring LinkedIn and GitHub to enhance its enterprise offerings.

Lessons Learned from Building a Tech Giant

Bill Gates' journey with Microsoft offers numerous lessons in leadership, innovation, and strategic management. Here are some key lessons learned from building a tech giant:

Vision and Foresight:

Seeing the Future: Gates' ability to envision the potential of personal computing and software development was a driving force behind Microsoft's success. His foresight allowed Microsoft to capitalize on emerging trends and technologies, staying ahead of the competition.

Adapting to Change: Gates recognized the importance of adapting to technological shifts, such as the transition from MS-DOS to Windows and the rise of the internet. This adaptability ensured Microsoft's continued relevance and growth in a rapidly evolving industry.

Innovation and Risk-Taking:

Embracing Innovation: Microsoft's success was built on a culture of innovation. Gates and his team were willing to take risks and experiment with new ideas, leading to groundbreaking products like Windows and Office.

Learning from Failure: Not all of Microsoft's initiatives were successful, but Gates viewed failures as learning opportunities. This mindset encouraged a continuous improvement approach, where setbacks were analyzed and used to inform future strategies.

Strategic Partnerships:

Leveraging Alliances: The partnership with IBM was a pivotal moment for Microsoft, providing the company with credibility and market access. Gates understood the value of strategic alliances and leveraged them to drive growth and expansion.

Balancing Competition and Collaboration: Gates navigated the fine line between competition and collaboration. While competing with other tech giants, Microsoft also collaborated with industry partners to enhance its offerings and reach new markets.

Customer Focus:

Understanding User Needs: Gates emphasized the importance of understanding and addressing user needs. Microsoft's success was built on developing products that were user-friendly, reliable, and met the demands of customers.

Continuous Improvement: Gates believed in the continuous improvement of products based on user feedback. This customer-centric approach helped Microsoft maintain its market leadership and build strong customer loyalty.

Leadership and Culture:

Empowering Teams: Gates fostered a culture of empowerment, encouraging employees to take initiative and innovate. He believed in hiring talented individuals and giving them the freedom to explore and create.

Setting High Standards: Gates set high standards for himself and his team. His pursuit of excellence drove Microsoft to achieve remarkable milestones and set industry standards.

Philanthropy and Social Responsibility:

Giving Back: Gates' success with Microsoft enabled him to focus on philanthropy and social responsibility. The establishment of the Bill & Melinda Gates Foundation reflects his commitment to using his resources and influence to address global challenges and improve lives.

Integrating Values: Gates' leadership at Microsoft was guided by a sense of responsibility and ethical conduct. This integration of values into business practices helped build a positive corporate reputation and trust with stakeholders.

In conclusion, the Microsoft era under Bill Gates' leadership is a testament to the power of vision, innovation, strategic thinking, and adaptability. The lessons learned from building Microsoft into a global tech giant provide valuable insights into effective leadership and management. Gates' journey highlights the importance of embracing change, fostering a culture of innovation, understanding customer needs, and balancing competition with collaboration. These lessons continue to inspire and guide leaders in the technology industry and beyond.

Chapter 5: Philanthropic Initiatives

The Bill & Melinda Gates Foundation

The Bill & Melinda Gates Foundation, established in 2000, is one of the largest and most influential philanthropic organizations in the world. With a mission to enhance the quality of life for individuals globally, the foundation focuses on critical areas such as global health, education, poverty alleviation, and social equity. Bill Gates and his then-wife, Melinda Gates, leveraged their wealth and influence to address some of the most pressing challenges facing humanity.

Foundation Overview:

Mission and Vision: The foundation aims to reduce inequities and improve the lives of the world's most vulnerable populations. Its guiding principle is that every life has equal value.

Funding and Resources: With an endowment of over $50 billion, the foundation has the financial resources to support large-scale initiatives and long-term projects. It partners with governments, NGOs, and private sector organizations to maximize its impact.

Impact on Global Health

The foundation's work in global health is perhaps its most transformative, addressing diseases that disproportionately affect the world's poorest populations and strengthening health systems.

Combating Infectious Diseases:

Polio Eradication: The foundation has been a key player in the global effort to eradicate polio. By funding vaccination campaigns, supporting surveillance systems, and advocating for global cooperation, it has helped reduce polio cases by over 99% since the late 1980s.

Malaria Control: The foundation has invested heavily in malaria prevention and treatment, funding the development of new drugs, insecticide-treated bed nets, and vaccines. These efforts have significantly reduced malaria mortality rates, particularly in sub-Saharan Africa.

HIV/AIDS: Through partnerships with organizations like the Global Fund and UNAIDS, the foundation has supported the distribution of antiretroviral therapy and prevention programs, contributing to a substantial decline in HIV/AIDS-related deaths.

Improving Maternal and Child Health:

Vaccination Programs: The foundation has played a pivotal role in increasing global vaccination coverage, preventing millions of deaths from diseases such as measles, pneumonia, and rotavirus. Initiatives like Gavi, the Vaccine Alliance, have been instrumental in these efforts.

Nutrition and Early Childhood Development: Recognizing the importance of the first 1,000 days of life, the foundation has funded programs to improve maternal nutrition, breastfeeding practices, and early childhood development, ensuring children have the best start in life.

Maternal Health: The foundation has worked to improve maternal health by supporting access to quality prenatal care, safe childbirth practices, and postpartum care. These efforts have led to significant reductions in maternal mortality in low-income countries.

Strengthening Health Systems:

Health Workforce Training: The foundation has invested in training healthcare workers, including doctors, nurses, and community health workers, to build local capacity and improve the quality of care.

Health Infrastructure: By funding the construction and renovation of health facilities, the foundation has improved access to healthcare services in underserved areas. It also supports the development of robust health information systems to enhance decision-making and resource allocation.

Impact on Education

The Gates Foundation has made substantial investments in education, with a focus on improving access, quality, and equity in both the United States and developing countries.

K-12 Education in the United States:

Common Core Standards: The foundation has been a major supporter of the Common Core State Standards, which aim to provide a consistent and high-quality education across states. These standards focus on critical thinking, problem-solving, and effective communication skills.

Teacher Effectiveness: The foundation has funded initiatives to improve teacher training, evaluation, and professional development. By enhancing the skills and support available to educators, it aims to improve student outcomes.

School Innovation: The foundation supports innovative school models, such as charter schools and personalized learning programs, to provide diverse educational options and meet the needs of all students.

Global Education:

Access to Education: In developing countries, the foundation works to increase access to education, particularly for girls and marginalized communities. This includes building schools, providing scholarships, and supporting initiatives to remove barriers to education.

Quality of Education: The foundation funds programs to improve the quality of education by developing effective curricula, training teachers, and integrating technology into classrooms. It also supports efforts to improve literacy and numeracy skills among young learners.

Higher Education and Vocational Training: The foundation supports higher education and vocational training programs to equip students with the skills needed for employment and economic self-sufficiency. This includes funding scholarships, building partnerships with universities, and supporting workforce development initiatives.

Impact on Poverty Alleviation

The Gates Foundation addresses poverty through a multifaceted approach, focusing on economic empowerment, agricultural development, and access to financial services.

Economic Empowerment:

Financial Inclusion: The foundation promotes financial inclusion by supporting the development of digital financial services, such as mobile banking and microfinance, which provide access to savings, credit, and insurance for underserved populations.

Women's Economic Empowerment: Recognizing the critical role of women in economic development, the foundation funds programs that promote women's economic empowerment through entrepreneurship, skills training, and access to financial resources.

Income Generation Programs: The foundation supports initiatives that create income-generating opportunities for low-income individuals and communities, such as small business development, vocational training, and job placement services.

Agricultural Development:

Smallholder Farmers: The foundation focuses on improving the productivity and livelihoods of smallholder farmers in developing countries. This includes funding research on high-yield and climate-resilient crops, providing access to quality seeds and fertilizers, and supporting agricultural extension services.

Sustainable Agriculture: The foundation promotes sustainable agricultural practices that increase productivity while protecting the environment. This includes supporting agroecological approaches, water conservation, and soil health initiatives.

Market Access: The foundation works to improve market access for smallholder farmers by supporting value chain development, infrastructure improvements, and market information systems. These efforts help farmers get fair prices for their produce and increase their income.

Addressing Urban Poverty:

Affordable Housing: The foundation supports efforts to increase the availability of affordable housing in urban areas. This includes funding the construction of low-cost housing units, supporting policies that promote affordable housing, and providing financial assistance to low-income families.

Urban Development: The foundation funds programs that address the challenges of urban poverty, such as slum upgrading, access to basic services, and social protection initiatives. These efforts aim to improve the living conditions and economic opportunities for urban poor communities.

Key Principles and Strategies

Evidence-Based Approach:

Data and Research: The foundation relies on data and rigorous research to inform its strategies and measure the impact of its initiatives. By investing in research and evaluation, it ensures that its programs are effective and scalable.

Learning and Adaptation: The foundation embraces a learning mindset, continuously assessing its work and adapting its strategies based on new evidence and changing circumstances. This approach allows it to remain flexible and responsive to emerging challenges and opportunities.

Partnership and Collaboration:

Global and Local Partnerships: The foundation collaborates with a wide range of partners, including governments, NGOs, private sector organizations, and communities. These partnerships enable it to leverage diverse expertise and resources, and to scale its impact.

Advocacy and Policy Engagement: The foundation engages in advocacy and policy work to influence public policies and mobilize resources for its priority areas. By working with policymakers and stakeholders, it aims to create an enabling environment for sustainable development.

Sustainability and Scalability:

Sustainable Solutions: The foundation prioritizes sustainable solutions that can be maintained and scaled over the long term. This includes building local capacity, promoting systemic change, and fostering community ownership of initiatives.

Scalable Models: The foundation seeks to identify and scale up successful models and best practices. By documenting and sharing lessons learned, it aims to replicate and expand effective interventions in different contexts.

In conclusion, the Bill & Melinda Gates Foundation has had a profound impact on global health, education, and poverty alleviation. Through its strategic investments and partnerships, it has improved the lives of millions of people worldwide. The foundation's work is guided by a commitment to equity, evidence-based decision-making, and collaboration. Its achievements in combating infectious diseases, improving maternal and child health, expanding access to education, and promoting economic empowerment demonstrate the power of philanthropy to drive positive change on a global scale. Bill Gates' leadership in this philanthropic endeavor reflects his dedication to using his wealth and influence to address some of the world's most pressing challenges and to create a more equitable and sustainable future.

Chapter 6: Global Influence

Gates' International Work and Influence

Bill Gates' international work extends beyond his role as a technology innovator and philanthropist. His global influence is a product of his extensive efforts to address critical global challenges through the Bill & Melinda Gates Foundation, his participation in international forums, and his collaborations with world leaders. This chapter explores the breadth of Gates' international work and how his global perspective could benefit U.S. foreign policy.

Global Health Initiatives:

Polio Eradication: Gates has been a key figure in the global campaign to eradicate polio, working closely with organizations like the World Health Organization (WHO), Rotary International, and UNICEF. His foundation has contributed billions of dollars to vaccination programs and surveillance efforts, significantly reducing polio cases worldwide.

HIV/AIDS, Malaria, and Tuberculosis: Gates has prioritized combating infectious diseases through funding for research, treatment, and prevention programs. His foundation supports the development of new vaccines, diagnostics, and treatments, and works with international partners to ensure access to these innovations in low-income countries.

Gavi, the Vaccine Alliance: As a major supporter of Gavi, the Gates Foundation has played a critical role in increasing immunization coverage in developing countries. This partnership has helped prevent millions of deaths from vaccine-preventable diseases and strengthened health systems globally.

Education and Development:

Global Education Initiatives: Gates' commitment to education extends internationally, with a focus on increasing access to quality education in low-income countries. The foundation supports programs that provide scholarships, build schools, and train teachers, particularly in regions where educational opportunities are limited.

Economic Development: Gates has worked to promote economic development through initiatives that support smallholder farmers, improve financial inclusion, and create job opportunities. His foundation's investments in agricultural research and development have helped increase food security and improve livelihoods in rural communities.

Climate Change and Sustainability:

Clean Energy Innovation: Gates is a strong advocate for addressing climate change through technological innovation. He has invested in clean energy solutions and supported initiatives like Breakthrough Energy Ventures, which funds startups developing sustainable technologies. His efforts aim to accelerate the transition to a low-carbon economy and mitigate the impacts of climate change.

Sustainable Development Goals (SDGs): Gates has been a vocal supporter of the United Nations' Sustainable Development Goals, which aim to address global challenges such as poverty, inequality, and environmental sustainability. His foundation aligns its work with these goals, contributing to global efforts to create a more sustainable and equitable world.

Global Advocacy and Policy Influence:

World Economic Forum: Gates is a regular participant in the World Economic Forum (WEF), where he engages with global leaders, policymakers, and business executives to discuss and address global challenges. His influence at the WEF and other international forums helps shape policies and mobilize resources for key issues.

Global Partnerships: Gates collaborates with international organizations, governments, and private sector partners to advance global health, education, and development agendas. His ability to convene diverse stakeholders and build coalitions has amplified the impact of his initiatives.

How His Global Perspective Could Benefit U.S. Foreign Policy

Bill Gates' extensive international work and global perspective position him uniquely to influence and enhance U.S. foreign policy. His understanding of global challenges, experience in building international partnerships, and commitment to sustainable development could bring significant benefits to America's approach to foreign policy.

Strengthening Global Health Security:

Pandemic Preparedness and Response: Gates' expertise in global health could inform U.S. strategies for pandemic preparedness and response. His experience with initiatives like the Coalition for Epidemic Preparedness Innovations (CEPI) and his advocacy for global health security would enhance the country's ability to respond to future health crises.

Global Health Diplomacy: Gates' relationships with international health organizations and his credibility in the global health community could facilitate stronger U.S. engagement in global health diplomacy. By prioritizing health initiatives, the U.S. could build goodwill and strengthen its leadership in addressing global health challenges.

Promoting Economic Development and Stability:

Aid and Development Programs: Gates' knowledge of effective development programs could inform U.S. foreign aid strategies, ensuring that resources are allocated to impactful initiatives. His focus on evidence-based approaches and sustainability would enhance the effectiveness of U.S. development assistance.

Economic Partnerships: Gates' work in promoting economic development through agriculture, financial inclusion, and clean energy aligns with U.S. interests in fostering global stability and prosperity. By supporting these initiatives, the U.S. could help create economic opportunities and reduce poverty in developing countries.

Addressing Climate Change:

Clean Energy and Innovation: Gates' commitment to clean energy innovation could drive U.S. leadership in addressing climate change. His support for research and development of sustainable technologies aligns with the need for global cooperation to mitigate climate impacts and transition to a low-carbon economy.

International Climate Agreements: Gates' influence could support U.S. efforts to engage in and lead international climate agreements, such as the Paris Agreement. His advocacy for ambitious climate action would strengthen the U.S. position in global climate negotiations.

Enhancing Global Education:

Education Diplomacy: Gates' initiatives in global education could inform U.S. policies to promote education as a tool for diplomacy and development. By investing in education programs, the U.S. could foster human capital development and support social and economic progress in partner countries.

Building Global Talent: Gates' emphasis on education and skills training aligns with the need to develop a global workforce capable of addressing future challenges. The U.S. could collaborate with international partners to enhance educational opportunities and build a talent pipeline for innovation and economic growth.

Promoting Multilateralism and Global Cooperation:

Building Alliances: Gates' ability to build and sustain international partnerships could support U.S. efforts to strengthen alliances and foster multilateral cooperation. His collaborative approach and commitment to common goals would enhance the U.S. role in addressing global challenges through collective action.

Advocating for Global Equity: Gates' advocacy for equity and inclusion aligns with U.S. values of promoting human rights and social justice. His influence could support U.S. efforts to address global inequities and champion policies that prioritize the needs of marginalized populations.

Leveraging Technology for Global Good:

Digital Diplomacy: Gates' background in technology and innovation could inform U.S. strategies for digital diplomacy. By leveraging technology to address global challenges, the U.S. could enhance its soft power and contribute to global progress in areas such as health, education, and economic development.

Cybersecurity and Global Governance: Gates' understanding of technology's impact on society could support U.S. efforts to address cybersecurity threats and promote global governance frameworks for the digital age. His insights would be valuable in shaping policies that protect digital infrastructure and ensure the responsible use of technology.

In conclusion, Bill Gates' global influence and extensive international work position him as a valuable asset for U.S. foreign policy. His experience in addressing global health challenges, promoting economic development, and advocating for sustainable development aligns with key U.S. interests. By leveraging Gates' global perspective and collaborative approach, the U.S. could enhance its leadership in addressing pressing global issues and fostering international cooperation. Gates' contributions to global health, education, and development demonstrate the potential for impactful and transformative foreign policy initiatives that prioritize the well-being of individuals worldwide.

Chapter 7: Economic Policy

Gates' Views on Economic Policy

Bill Gates' perspective on economic policy is deeply influenced by his experience as a tech entrepreneur, philanthropist, and advocate for sustainable development. His approach combines innovation, equity, and long-term planning, emphasizing the importance of investing in technology, education, and infrastructure to drive economic growth and address systemic challenges.

Innovation and Technology:

Investment in R&D: Gates strongly advocates for increased investment in research and development (R&D) to drive innovation. He believes that technological advancements are crucial for solving complex problems and maintaining economic competitiveness. This includes funding for emerging technologies such as artificial intelligence, biotechnology, and clean energy.

Digital Economy: Gates supports the expansion of the digital economy, recognizing its potential to create new job opportunities and drive economic growth. He emphasizes the importance of digital infrastructure, including broadband access and cybersecurity, to ensure that all citizens can participate in and benefit from the digital economy.

Education and Workforce Development:

STEM Education: Gates emphasizes the importance of science, technology, engineering, and mathematics (STEM) education to prepare the workforce for the demands of the 21st century. He advocates for educational reforms that prioritize STEM subjects, as well as initiatives to close the skills gap and promote lifelong learning.

Vocational Training: Gates supports vocational training programs that equip individuals with the skills needed for high-demand jobs. He believes that such programs can provide pathways to economic mobility and help address unemployment and underemployment.

Economic Equity:

Progressive Taxation: Gates has expressed support for a progressive taxation system, where the wealthy pay a higher share of their income in taxes. He believes that this approach can help address income inequality and generate revenue for social programs and public investments.

Social Safety Nets: Gates advocates for robust social safety nets, including healthcare, unemployment benefits, and social security, to protect vulnerable populations and reduce economic disparities. He supports policies that ensure access to basic services and promote economic security for all citizens.

Climate Change and Sustainability:

Green Economy: Gates is a strong proponent of transitioning to a green economy, which involves investing in renewable energy, sustainable agriculture, and other environmentally friendly practices. He believes that addressing climate change is not only a moral imperative but also an economic opportunity to create new industries and jobs.

Carbon Pricing: Gates supports carbon pricing mechanisms, such as carbon taxes or cap-and-trade systems, to incentivize reductions in greenhouse gas emissions. He believes that putting a price on carbon can drive innovation in clean energy and help mitigate the impacts of climate change.

Infrastructure Investment:

Modernization of Infrastructure: Gates advocates for significant investments in modernizing infrastructure, including transportation, energy, and water systems. He believes that upgrading infrastructure is essential for economic growth, public safety, and environmental sustainability.

Public-Private Partnerships: Gates supports public-private partnerships to leverage private sector expertise and resources in infrastructure projects. He believes that such collaborations can enhance efficiency and innovation in the development and maintenance of critical infrastructure.

How He Would Address Economic Challenges

If Bill Gates were to run for and become President, his approach to addressing economic challenges would likely involve a combination of innovative policies, strategic investments, and collaborative efforts. His economic agenda would focus on fostering sustainable growth, reducing inequality, and ensuring long-term prosperity.

Tackling Income Inequality:

Progressive Tax Reforms: Gates would likely implement progressive tax reforms to ensure that the wealthy pay a fair share of taxes. This could include higher taxes on capital gains, estates, and large inheritances, as well as closing tax loopholes that benefit the ultra-rich.

Raising the Minimum Wage: Gates would support efforts to raise the federal minimum wage to a livable level, ensuring that workers can earn enough to support themselves and their families. He would also advocate for policies that promote fair labor practices and protect workers' rights.

Expanding Access to Education and Training: By investing in education and vocational training programs, Gates would aim to provide individuals with the skills needed to secure well-paying jobs. This would include support for community colleges, apprenticeships, and on-the-job training programs.

Promoting Sustainable Economic Growth:

Investment in Clean Energy: Gates would prioritize investments in clean energy technologies, such as wind, solar, and advanced nuclear power. He would support policies that encourage the adoption of renewable energy and the development of innovative solutions to reduce carbon emissions.

Support for Research and Development: Gates would advocate for increased funding for R&D across various sectors, including healthcare, technology, and environmental science. He believes that such investments are crucial for driving innovation, improving productivity, and maintaining global competitiveness.

Infrastructure Modernization: Gates would push for a comprehensive infrastructure plan to modernize transportation networks, energy grids, and water systems. This would involve leveraging public-private partnerships to finance and implement infrastructure projects efficiently.

Addressing Climate Change:

Carbon Pricing Mechanisms: Gates would likely implement carbon pricing mechanisms to reduce greenhouse gas emissions. This could include a carbon tax or cap-and-trade system to incentivize businesses to adopt cleaner practices and invest in sustainable technologies.

Green Jobs and Economic Transition: Gates would support policies that facilitate a just transition to a green economy, ensuring that workers in traditional industries are not left behind. This could involve retraining programs, job placement services, and support for communities affected by the shift to renewable energy.

Global Leadership on Climate Action: Gates would advocate for the U.S. to take a leading role in international climate negotiations and agreements. He believes that global cooperation is essential for addressing climate change and promoting sustainable development.

Enhancing Economic Resilience:

Strengthening Social Safety Nets: Gates would work to strengthen social safety nets, including healthcare, unemployment benefits, and social security. He believes that robust safety nets are essential for protecting individuals and families during economic downturns and promoting economic stability.

Promoting Economic Diversification: Gates would support policies that promote economic diversification, reducing reliance on any single industry or sector. This would involve investing in emerging industries, supporting small businesses, and fostering innovation and entrepreneurship.

Fiscal Responsibility: Gates would advocate for fiscal responsibility, ensuring that government spending is efficient and sustainable. He would prioritize investments that yield long-term economic benefits and work to reduce the federal deficit through balanced budgeting.

Fostering Global Competitiveness:

Trade Policies and Global Partnerships: Gates would support fair trade policies that promote global economic cooperation and benefit American workers and businesses. He would advocate for trade agreements that protect intellectual property, promote environmental standards, and ensure labor rights.

Investing in Innovation Hubs: Gates would encourage the development of innovation hubs and technology clusters to attract talent, investment, and businesses. These hubs would serve as centers of excellence for research, development, and commercialization of new technologies.

Enhancing Workforce Mobility: Gates would support policies that enhance workforce mobility, allowing individuals to move freely between jobs and regions. This could involve portable benefits, retraining programs, and support for remote work and telecommuting.

In my conclusion, Bill Gates' views on economic policy reflect his commitment to innovation, equity, and sustainability. His approach to addressing economic challenges would involve strategic investments in technology, education, and infrastructure, as well as policies that promote economic equity and resilience. By leveraging his experience as a tech entrepreneur and philanthropist, Gates would aim to foster sustainable economic growth, reduce inequality, and ensure long-term prosperity for all Americans. His leadership in economic policy would prioritize innovation, collaboration, and evidence-based decision-making, positioning the U.S. to address current challenges and seize future opportunities.

Chapter 8: Education Reform

Gates' Contributions to Education

Bill Gates has long been a champion of education reform, dedicating significant resources and effort through the Bill & Melinda Gates Foundation. His contributions to education focus on improving access, quality, and outcomes for students across the globe, with a particular emphasis on underserved and marginalized communities.

Investment in K-12 Education:

Teacher Effectiveness: Gates has prioritized enhancing teacher effectiveness as a cornerstone of improving K-12 education. The foundation has invested in programs that provide professional development, mentorship, and evaluation systems to help teachers improve their instructional practices.

Common Core Standards: Gates has been a strong supporter of the Common Core State Standards, which aim to provide consistent, high-quality education standards across states. The foundation has funded initiatives to develop and implement these standards, focusing on critical thinking and problem-solving skills.

Innovative Schools: Gates has funded and supported innovative school models, including charter schools and personalized learning environments. These schools often use technology and data to tailor instruction to individual student needs, promoting student engagement and achievement.

Higher Education:

College Access and Completion: Gates has focused on increasing college access and completion rates, particularly for low-income and minority students. The foundation supports programs that provide financial aid, academic support, and college counseling to help students enroll in and complete postsecondary education.

Community Colleges: Recognizing the importance of community colleges in providing affordable education and workforce training, Gates has invested in initiatives to improve student success at these institutions. This includes efforts to streamline transfer pathways, enhance advising, and develop competency-based education models.

Online Learning and Innovation: Gates has been a proponent of leveraging technology to expand access to higher education. The foundation has supported the development of online learning platforms and innovative educational technologies that provide flexible, high-quality learning opportunities.

Global Education Initiatives:

Access to Quality Education: Gates has worked to increase access to quality education in low-income countries, focusing on improving learning outcomes for children in these regions. The foundation funds programs that build schools, train teachers, and develop educational materials.

Educational Equity: Gates has advocated for educational equity, supporting initiatives that address disparities in education access and quality. This includes efforts to ensure that girls, children with disabilities, and other marginalized groups have the opportunity to receive a quality education.

His Plans for Improving the U.S. Education System

If Bill Gates were to become President, his plans for improving the U.S. education system would likely build on his extensive experience and successful initiatives. His approach would focus on addressing systemic challenges, promoting innovation, and ensuring that all students have access to a high-quality education.

Enhancing Teacher Quality and Support:

Professional Development: Gates would prioritize comprehensive professional development for teachers, providing ongoing training and support to help them improve their instructional practices. This would include mentoring programs, collaborative learning communities, and access to high-quality resources.

Evaluation and Feedback Systems: Gates would advocate for the implementation of robust evaluation and feedback systems that help teachers identify areas for improvement and celebrate their successes. These systems would use multiple measures, including student growth, peer observations, and self-assessments.

Teacher Compensation: Recognizing the importance of attracting and retaining talented educators, Gates would support efforts to improve teacher compensation and working conditions. This could include performance-based pay, career advancement opportunities, and incentives for teaching in high-need areas.

Expanding Access to Early Childhood Education:

Universal Pre-K: Gates would likely advocate for the expansion of universal pre-kindergarten programs to ensure that all children have access to high-quality early childhood education. Research shows that early education is crucial for cognitive and social development and can have long-term benefits for academic success.

Early Literacy and Numeracy Programs: Gates would support initiatives that focus on developing early literacy and numeracy skills, providing children with a strong foundation for future learning. This could include funding for preschool programs, parent education, and community partnerships.

Promoting Equity and Inclusion:

Addressing Disparities: Gates would prioritize addressing disparities in education access and outcomes, ensuring that all students, regardless of their background, have the opportunity to succeed. This would involve targeted support for low-income students, students of color, English language learners, and students with disabilities.

Community Schools: Gates would likely support the development of community schools that provide comprehensive services to students and their families. These schools would offer health and social services, after-school programs, and family engagement initiatives to address barriers to learning.

Leveraging Technology for Personalized Learning:

Technology Integration: Gates would advocate for the integration of technology in classrooms to support personalized learning. This approach tailors instruction to individual student needs, using data and adaptive learning technologies to provide targeted support and enrichment.

Digital Literacy: Recognizing the importance of digital literacy in the modern economy, Gates would support initiatives to ensure that all students have access to technology and the skills needed to use it effectively. This could include funding for device access, broadband connectivity, and digital literacy curricula.

Strengthening Higher Education and Workforce Development:

College Affordability: Gates would work to make higher education more affordable, supporting efforts to reduce tuition costs, increase financial aid, and address student debt. This could involve expanding Pell Grants, implementing income-driven repayment plans, and promoting cost-saving innovations in higher education.

Workforce Alignment: Gates would advocate for stronger alignment between education and workforce needs, ensuring that students are prepared for high-demand careers. This would involve partnerships with industry, development of career and technical education programs, and support for apprenticeships and internships.

Fostering Innovation in Education:

R&D in Education: Gates would likely support increased investment in research and development in education, promoting the use of evidence-based practices and innovative approaches. This could include funding for educational research, pilot programs, and scaling of successful initiatives.

Public-Private Partnerships: Gates would encourage public-private partnerships to bring innovative solutions to education challenges. By leveraging the expertise and resources of the private sector, the U.S. could accelerate the development and implementation of new educational technologies and models.

Improving School Infrastructure:

Modernizing Facilities: Gates would prioritize the modernization of school facilities, ensuring that students have access to safe, healthy, and conducive learning environments. This could involve funding for renovations, construction of new schools, and upgrades to technology infrastructure.

Sustainable Practices: Gates would advocate for the adoption of sustainable practices in schools, promoting energy efficiency, use of renewable energy, and green building standards. This approach not only benefits the environment but also provides educational opportunities for students.

Bill Gates' contributions to education have demonstrated his commitment to improving educational access, quality, and outcomes. His plans for the U.S. education system would build on this experience, focusing on enhancing teacher quality, expanding early childhood education, promoting equity, leveraging technology, strengthening higher education, fostering innovation, and improving school infrastructure.

Gates' vision for education reform emphasizes the importance of evidence-based practices, collaboration, and long-term planning, aiming to create an education system that prepares all students for success in the 21st century. As President, his leadership in education reform would prioritize innovation, equity, and sustainability, positioning the U.S. to address current challenges and seize future opportunities in education.

Chapter 9: Healthcare Innovation

Gates' Work in Global Health

Bill Gates' contributions to global health have been transformative, driven primarily through the Bill & Melinda Gates Foundation. His work has focused on combating infectious diseases, improving maternal and child health, and strengthening health systems worldwide.

Combating Infectious Diseases:

Vaccination Programs: One of Gates' most significant contributions to global health has been in the area of vaccination. The foundation has funded the development and distribution of vaccines for diseases like polio, malaria, and HIV. Notably, the foundation has been a key player in the global effort to eradicate polio, significantly reducing the number of cases worldwide.

Malaria and Tuberculosis: Gates has invested heavily in the fight against malaria and tuberculosis, funding research to develop new treatments and preventative measures.

This includes support for innovative technologies such as genetically modified mosquitoes to reduce malaria transmission and new drug regimens for tuberculosis.

Maternal and Child Health:

Nutrition and Immunization: The Gates Foundation has worked to improve maternal and child health by funding programs that provide essential nutrition and immunization services. This includes initiatives to promote breastfeeding, provide micronutrient supplements, and ensure that children receive necessary vaccinations.

Family Planning: Gates has also supported family planning initiatives to help women access contraception and reproductive health services. This effort aims to reduce maternal and child mortality by allowing women to space and plan their pregnancies.

Strengthening Health Systems:

Health Infrastructure: Gates has funded projects to strengthen health infrastructure in low-income countries, including the construction of clinics, training of healthcare workers, and development of health information systems. These efforts aim to improve the capacity of health systems to deliver quality care.

Data and Technology: Recognizing the importance of data in improving health outcomes, Gates has supported the development of health information systems that collect and analyze data on disease prevalence, treatment outcomes, and healthcare delivery. This information is used to inform policy decisions and allocate resources more effectively.

Research and Development:

Innovative Health Technologies: Gates has been a proponent of investing in research and development to create innovative health technologies. This includes funding for new diagnostic tools, treatments, and vaccines, as well as support for scientific research to better understand diseases and their transmission.

Global Health Partnerships: Gates has fostered partnerships with governments, international organizations, and the private sector to tackle global health challenges. These collaborations have led to coordinated efforts in disease eradication, health system strengthening, and the development of new health interventions.

Proposals for Reforming the U.S. Healthcare System

Drawing on his global health experience, Bill Gates' proposals for reforming the U.S. healthcare system would likely emphasize innovation, equity, and sustainability. His approach would focus on expanding access to care, improving health outcomes, and reducing costs through strategic investments and policy changes.

Expanding Access to Care:

Universal Coverage: Gates would likely advocate for a system of universal healthcare coverage, ensuring that all Americans have access to essential health services. This could involve expanding existing programs like Medicaid and Medicare or implementing a public option that provides affordable coverage to those who are uninsured or underinsured.

Primary Care: Recognizing the importance of primary care in preventing and managing chronic conditions, Gates would support initiatives to expand access to primary care services. This could include funding for community health centers, incentives for primary care providers, and efforts to integrate primary care with other health services.

Improving Health Outcomes:

Preventive Care: Gates would emphasize the importance of preventive care in improving health outcomes and reducing healthcare costs. This would involve expanding access to preventive services such as vaccinations, screenings, and wellness programs, as well as promoting healthy behaviors through public health campaigns.

Chronic Disease Management: Gates would support efforts to improve the management of chronic diseases such as diabetes, heart disease, and asthma. This could include funding for disease management programs, patient education initiatives, and the use of technology to monitor and support patients' health.

Reducing Healthcare Costs:

Value-Based Care: Gates would likely advocate for a shift toward value-based care, where providers are reimbursed based on patient outcomes rather than the volume of services provided. This approach incentivizes high-quality, cost-effective care and can lead to better health outcomes and lower costs.

Pharmaceutical Pricing: Gates would support policies to reduce the cost of prescription drugs, such as allowing Medicare to negotiate drug prices, promoting the use of generic and biosimilar medications, and increasing transparency in drug pricing.

Investing in Health Innovation:

Research and Development: Gates would prioritize investment in health research and development, supporting the creation of new treatments, diagnostics, and technologies. This could involve increased funding for the National Institutes of Health (NIH), public-private partnerships, and incentives for innovation in the pharmaceutical and biotechnology industries.

Health Technology: Gates would advocate for the adoption of health technology to improve care delivery and patient outcomes. This could include the use of electronic health records, telemedicine, and data analytics to enhance clinical decision-making and streamline healthcare operations.

Addressing Social Determinants of Health:

Integrated Care: Gates would support efforts to address social determinants of health, recognizing that factors such as housing, education, and income have a significant impact on health outcomes. This could involve integrating health and social services, promoting cross-sector collaboration, and funding programs that address the root causes of health disparities.

Community Health Initiatives: Gates would likely advocate for community health initiatives that engage local organizations and stakeholders in promoting health and wellness. This could include funding for community-based health programs, support for health education and outreach, and partnerships with local governments and non-profits.

Strengthening the Healthcare Workforce:

Workforce Training and Development: Gates would prioritize the training and development of the healthcare workforce to ensure that there are enough skilled professionals to meet the needs of the population. This could involve funding for medical and nursing schools, support for continuing education and professional development, and incentives to work in underserved areas.

Team-Based Care: Gates would support models of team-based care that involve a multidisciplinary approach to patient care. This could include the use of nurse practitioners, physician assistants, and other healthcare professionals to provide comprehensive, coordinated care.

Bill Gates' extensive work in global health has provided him with a deep understanding of the challenges and opportunities in healthcare. His proposals for reforming the U.S. healthcare system would build on this experience, focusing on expanding access to care, improving health outcomes, reducing costs, and investing in innovation. Gates' vision for healthcare reform emphasizes the importance of preventive care, chronic disease management, value-based care, and addressing social determinants of health.

By leveraging technology, fostering collaboration, and promoting equity, Gates would aim to create a healthcare system that is efficient, effective, and accessible to all Americans. As President, his leadership in healthcare innovation would prioritize long-term solutions, ensuring that the U.S. healthcare system can meet the needs of its population and adapt to future challenges.

Chapter 10: Technology and Innovation

Gates' Expertise in Technology

Bill Gates' expertise in technology is rooted in his experience as a co-founder of Microsoft and his subsequent work as a technology advocate and philanthropist. His deep understanding of technology and its potential for societal impact has shaped his approach to fostering innovation and improving digital infrastructure.

Founding Microsoft:

Software Revolution: Gates co-founded Microsoft in 1975, a pivotal moment in the software revolution. His vision was to make computing accessible to individuals and businesses, leading to the development of the MS-DOS operating system and later the Windows operating system, which became the dominant platform for personal computers. This achievement transformed the technology landscape and set the stage for widespread digital adoption.

Product Development: Under Gates' leadership, Microsoft developed a range of products that revolutionized the software industry, including Microsoft Office, a suite of productivity tools that remains widely used today. Gates' focus on user-friendly software and robust business applications helped establish Microsoft as a tech giant.

Philanthropic Efforts in Technology:

Technology for Global Health: Gates has leveraged technology to address global health challenges through the Bill & Melinda Gates Foundation. This includes funding the development of new diagnostics, treatments, and vaccines, as well as supporting digital health initiatives such as electronic medical records and telemedicine in low-resource settings.

Education Technology: Gates has supported the use of technology in education to improve learning outcomes. This includes funding for educational software, online learning platforms, and data-driven approaches to personalized learning.

Advocacy for Technology Innovation:

Emerging Technologies: Gates is a vocal advocate for emerging technologies such as artificial intelligence, biotechnology, and clean energy. He emphasizes the potential of these technologies to solve complex problems and drive economic growth.

Public and Private Sector Collaboration: Gates has championed collaborations between the public and private sectors to advance technological innovation. This includes partnerships with governments, research institutions, and private companies to tackle global challenges and accelerate the development of new technologies.

How He Would Promote Innovation and Digital Infrastructure

If Bill Gates were to become President, his approach to promoting innovation and enhancing digital infrastructure would likely draw on his extensive experience in technology and his commitment to leveraging technology for societal benefit. His strategy would focus on fostering a conducive environment for innovation, investing in digital infrastructure, and addressing key challenges in technology adoption and development.

Fostering a Conducive Environment for Innovation:

Investment in R&D: Gates would prioritize increased investment in research and development to drive technological innovation. This could involve funding for basic research, applied research, and the commercialization of new technologies. He would support initiatives that encourage collaboration between academia, industry, and government agencies.

Startup Ecosystem: Gates would advocate for policies that support the startup ecosystem, including access to venture capital, incubators, and accelerators. By fostering an environment that nurtures entrepreneurship and innovation, Gates aims to stimulate the development of new technologies and business models.

Regulatory Framework: Gates would work to create a regulatory framework that balances innovation with safety and ethical considerations. This includes developing policies that encourage innovation while addressing issues such as data privacy, cybersecurity, and the ethical implications of emerging technologies.

Investing in Digital Infrastructure:

Broadband Access: Gates would prioritize expanding broadband access to ensure that all Americans have reliable internet connectivity. This would involve investing in infrastructure to provide high-speed internet to underserved and rural areas, promoting digital inclusion, and supporting initiatives to bridge the digital divide.

Smart Cities: Gates would support the development of smart cities that leverage technology to improve urban living. This includes investments in smart infrastructure such as sensors, data analytics, and IoT (Internet of Things) technologies to enhance transportation, energy management, and public services.

Cybersecurity: Recognizing the importance of cybersecurity in protecting digital infrastructure, Gates would advocate for increased investment in cybersecurity measures. This includes funding for research and development in cybersecurity technologies, enhancing public-private partnerships, and implementing robust security protocols to protect against cyber threats.

Promoting Technology Education and Workforce Development:

STEM Education: Gates would emphasize the importance of science, technology, engineering, and mathematics (STEM) education to prepare the workforce for the demands of the technology sector. This includes supporting K-12 education initiatives, funding scholarships and grants for STEM students, and promoting pathways to technology careers.

Reskilling and Upskilling: Gates would support programs that provide reskilling and upskilling opportunities for workers in response to technological changes. This includes funding for workforce training programs, vocational education, and partnerships with technology companies to provide on-the-job training and apprenticeships.

Encouraging Technological Innovation in Key Sectors:

Healthcare Innovation: Gates would advocate for the application of technology to improve healthcare outcomes. This includes supporting innovations in digital health, telemedicine, and personalized medicine, as well as funding research on new treatments and medical technologies.

Clean Energy: Gates would promote the development and adoption of clean energy technologies to address climate change and reduce reliance on fossil fuels. This includes funding for research in renewable energy, energy storage, and energy efficiency, as well as supporting policies that incentivize the adoption of clean energy solutions.

Agriculture Technology: Gates would support the use of technology to improve agricultural productivity and sustainability. This includes funding for precision agriculture, crop monitoring technologies, and advancements in agricultural research to enhance food security and reduce environmental impact.

Enhancing Data and Analytics Capabilities:

Data-Driven Decision Making: Gates would advocate for the use of data and analytics to inform policy decisions and improve government operations. This includes investing in data infrastructure, developing data-sharing frameworks, and promoting transparency and accountability in data collection and use.

AI and Machine Learning: Gates would support the development and application of artificial intelligence (AI) and machine learning to solve complex problems and drive innovation. This includes funding research on AI applications, promoting ethical AI practices, and supporting initiatives that use AI to address societal challenges.

1. **Global Collaboration and Leadership:**
    - **International Partnerships:** Gates would emphasize the importance of international collaboration in advancing technology and addressing global challenges. This includes fostering partnerships with other countries, international organizations, and multinational companies to drive innovation and address issues such as global health, climate change, and cybersecurity.
    - **Global Technology Standards:** Gates would support the development of global technology standards to ensure interoperability, security, and privacy. This includes participating in international forums and agreements to establish standards for emerging technologies and promote best practices.

Bill Gates' expertise in technology and his commitment to leveraging technology for societal benefit would shape his approach to promoting innovation and enhancing digital infrastructure as President. His strategy would involve increasing investment in R&D, supporting the startup ecosystem, expanding broadband access, investing in smart cities, and enhancing cybersecurity. Gates would also focus on technology education and workforce development, encouraging innovation in key sectors such as healthcare, clean energy, and agriculture, and leveraging data and analytics for decision-making.

By fostering a conducive environment for innovation and addressing key challenges in technology adoption, Gates aims to drive technological progress and ensure that the benefits of technology are widely shared. His leadership in technology and innovation would prioritize long-term solutions, global collaboration, and a focus on addressing pressing societal issues through technological advancements.

Chapter 11: Climate Change

Gates' Commitment to Addressing Climate Change

Bill Gates has been a prominent advocate for addressing climate change, recognizing it as one of the most pressing global challenges. His commitment is reflected in his philanthropic work, public advocacy, and investment in innovative solutions to reduce greenhouse gas emissions and promote sustainable development.

Philanthropic Initiatives:

Breakthrough Energy Ventures: Gates co-founded Breakthrough Energy Ventures (BEV) to support innovative technologies and companies that aim to reduce greenhouse gas emissions. BEV focuses on investing in breakthrough technologies across various sectors, including energy, transportation, agriculture, and manufacturing.

The Bill & Melinda Gates Foundation: While the foundation's primary focus is on global health and development, it has also supported climate-related initiatives. This includes funding research on sustainable agriculture, clean energy, and innovations to help developing countries adapt to climate change.

Advocacy and Public Engagement:

Books and Publications: Gates has authored books and articles highlighting the urgency of climate action and the need for technological innovation. His book "How to Avoid a Climate Disaster" provides a comprehensive overview of the climate crisis and practical solutions to address it.

Public Speaking: Gates frequently speaks at international conferences, forums, and media platforms to raise awareness about climate change and advocate for effective climate policies. He emphasizes the importance of global cooperation and the role of technology in mitigating climate impacts.

Policy Recommendations:

Innovative Policies: Gates has advocated for policies that support innovation and accelerate the transition to a low-carbon economy. This includes advocating for carbon pricing, government funding for research and development, and international agreements to reduce emissions.

Global Collaboration: Gates emphasizes the need for international collaboration to tackle climate change, supporting global agreements such as the Paris Agreement and encouraging countries to commit to ambitious climate targets.

His Plans for Sustainable Energy and Environmental Policies

If Bill Gates were to become President, his approach to addressing climate change would likely be comprehensive and multifaceted, drawing on his expertise in technology and his commitment to sustainability. His plans would focus on promoting sustainable energy, implementing environmental policies, and fostering innovation to achieve long-term climate goals.

Promoting Sustainable Energy:

Investment in Clean Energy Technologies:

Renewable Energy: Gates would prioritize investments in renewable energy sources such as solar, wind, and geothermal power. This includes funding research to improve the efficiency and affordability of renewable technologies, as well as supporting large-scale deployment projects.

Energy Storage: Recognizing the importance of energy storage in enabling a reliable and resilient renewable energy grid, Gates would support advancements in battery technology and other energy storage solutions. This includes funding research on new storage materials and technologies.

Next-Generation Nuclear Power: Gates has expressed support for next-generation nuclear power technologies, such as small modular reactors (SMRs) and advanced reactors. He would advocate for investments in these technologies to provide a low-carbon energy option with enhanced safety and efficiency.

Supporting Energy Efficiency:

Building Standards: Gates would promote the adoption of stringent energy efficiency standards for buildings and infrastructure. This includes incentivizing retrofits and upgrades to improve energy performance and reduce greenhouse gas emissions from the built environment.

Industrial Processes: Gates would support initiatives to improve energy efficiency in industrial processes, including funding for research on low-carbon manufacturing techniques and technologies that reduce emissions from heavy industries.

Encouraging Electrification:

Transportation Electrification: Gates would advocate for the electrification of transportation systems, including electric vehicles (EVs) and public transit. This includes supporting policies that promote EV adoption, build charging infrastructure, and incentivize the development of electric transportation technologies.

Heat Electrification: Gates would support efforts to electrify heating systems in homes and businesses, replacing fossil fuel-based heating with electric heat pumps and other low-carbon technologies.

Implementing Environmental Policies:

Carbon Pricing and Emissions Reduction:

Carbon Tax or Cap-and-Trade: Gates would support the implementation of a carbon pricing mechanism, such as a carbon tax or cap-and-trade system, to incentivize emissions reductions and internalize the environmental costs of greenhouse gas emissions.

Emissions Standards: Gates would advocate for stringent emissions standards for key sectors, including power generation, transportation, and industry. This includes setting ambitious targets for reducing greenhouse gas emissions and implementing regulations to achieve these targets.

Conservation and Land Use:

Protecting Ecosystems: Gates would prioritize the protection and restoration of natural ecosystems, including forests, wetlands, and grasslands. This includes supporting conservation initiatives, reforestation projects, and policies that prevent habitat destruction.

Sustainable Agriculture: Gates would support sustainable agricultural practices that reduce greenhouse gas emissions, improve soil health, and enhance resilience to climate change. This includes funding for research on climate-smart agriculture and promoting practices such as precision farming and agroforestry.

Climate Resilience and Adaptation:

Infrastructure Resilience: Gates would advocate for investments in infrastructure that enhances resilience to climate impacts, such as flood defenses, heat-resistant building materials, and climate-resilient transportation systems.

Disaster Preparedness: Gates would support policies and programs that improve preparedness and response to climate-related disasters, including funding for early warning systems, emergency response plans, and community-based adaptation initiatives.

Fostering Innovation and Research:

Funding Research and Development:

Climate Solutions: Gates would prioritize funding for research and development of innovative climate solutions. This includes supporting scientific research on new technologies, materials, and approaches to reduce greenhouse gas emissions and adapt to climate change.

Public-Private Partnerships: Gates would encourage public-private partnerships to accelerate the development and deployment of climate technologies. This includes collaborating with private companies, research institutions, and non-governmental organizations to advance innovative solutions.

Encouraging Technological Advancements:

Green Tech Startups: Gates would support the growth of green tech startups that are developing cutting-edge technologies to address climate challenges. This includes providing funding, mentorship, and resources to help startups scale their innovations.

Tech Innovation Hubs: Gates would promote the establishment of innovation hubs and research centers focused on climate technology. These centers would serve as collaborative spaces for researchers, entrepreneurs, and policymakers to develop and test new solutions.

Promoting International Cooperation:

Global Climate Agreements: Gates would support international climate agreements and efforts to achieve global climate goals. This includes participating in and promoting the implementation of agreements such as the Paris Agreement and encouraging countries to set and meet ambitious climate targets.

Technology Transfer: Gates would advocate for technology transfer to support climate action in developing countries. This includes facilitating the sharing of clean energy technologies, providing financial and technical assistance, and supporting capacity-building initiatives.

Bill Gates' commitment to addressing climate change is reflected in his philanthropic work, public advocacy, and investment in innovative solutions. His plans for sustainable energy and environmental policies as President would focus on promoting clean energy technologies, improving energy efficiency, and implementing robust environmental policies.

Gates would prioritize investments in research and development, support the electrification of transportation and heating, and advocate for carbon pricing and emissions reduction. His approach would also emphasize conservation, climate resilience, and international cooperation, aiming to drive technological innovation and achieve long-term climate goals. Gates' leadership in climate action would seek to address the urgent challenges of climate change while promoting a sustainable and equitable future for all.

Chapter 12: Social Justice and Equality

Gates' Stance on Social Justice Issues

Bill Gates has consistently expressed a strong commitment to social justice and equality, both through his philanthropic work and public advocacy. His stance on these issues is rooted in a belief that addressing inequality and promoting justice are fundamental to creating a better, more equitable society.

Philanthropic Efforts:

Bill & Melinda Gates Foundation: Through the Gates Foundation, Gates has supported numerous initiatives aimed at improving social justice and reducing inequality. The foundation's work spans global health, education, and poverty alleviation, all of which are interconnected with issues of social justice and equality.

Focus on Disadvantaged Communities: Gates has emphasized the importance of targeting efforts toward the most disadvantaged and marginalized communities. This includes supporting programs that address the needs of women and girls, racial and ethnic minorities, and economically disadvantaged populations.

Public Advocacy:

Promoting Equity: Gates has used his platform to advocate for policies and practices that promote equity and social justice. He has spoken out on issues such as income inequality, racial disparities, and access to education and healthcare.

Educational Inequality: Gates has highlighted the need to address disparities in educational opportunities and outcomes. He has supported initiatives aimed at closing the education gap and ensuring that all students, regardless of their background, have access to high-quality education.

Commitment to Diversity and Inclusion:

Diversity in Philanthropy: Gates has promoted diversity and inclusion within the philanthropic sector, advocating for more inclusive practices and greater representation of marginalized groups in decision-making processes.

Corporate Social Responsibility: Gates has also emphasized the importance of diversity and inclusion in the corporate world, advocating for policies and practices that promote fairness and equal opportunities in the workplace.

Policies to Promote Equality and Justice

As President, Bill Gates would likely implement a range of policies aimed at promoting social justice and equality. His approach would focus on addressing systemic inequalities, supporting marginalized communities, and ensuring that all individuals have equal opportunities to succeed.

Addressing Systemic Inequalities:

Income Inequality:

Progressive Taxation: Gates would support progressive tax policies designed to address income inequality. This includes advocating for higher tax rates on the wealthy and implementing measures to ensure that the tax system is equitable and fair.

Minimum Wage Increases: Gates would support raising the federal minimum wage to ensure that all workers earn a living wage that reflects the cost of living. This includes advocating for policies that address wage stagnation and promote fair compensation.

Affordable Housing:

Housing Assistance Programs: Gates would prioritize expanding affordable housing programs to ensure that low-income individuals and families have access to safe and affordable housing. This includes increasing funding for housing vouchers, subsidies, and public housing initiatives.

Housing Equity: Gates would support policies aimed at addressing housing discrimination and promoting fair housing practices. This includes enforcing anti-discrimination laws and supporting initiatives that prevent displacement and gentrification.

Supporting Marginalized Communities:

Racial and Ethnic Equity:

Criminal Justice Reform: Gates would advocate for comprehensive criminal justice reform to address racial disparities and ensure that the justice system is fair and equitable. This includes supporting reforms to reduce mass incarceration, eliminate racial profiling, and improve police-community relations.

Economic Empowerment: Gates would support initiatives to promote economic empowerment and wealth-building opportunities for racial and ethnic minorities. This includes funding for minority-owned businesses, entrepreneurship programs, and financial literacy education.

Gender Equality:

Equal Pay: Gates would advocate for policies that address the gender pay gap and ensure that women receive equal pay for equal work. This includes supporting pay transparency initiatives and enforcing equal pay laws.

Support for Women and Girls: Gates would prioritize policies that support women and girls in various aspects of life, including access to education, healthcare, and economic opportunities. This includes funding programs that address gender-based violence, reproductive health, and leadership development for women and girls.

Ensuring Equal Opportunities:

Education:

Equitable Education Funding: Gates would support reforms to ensure equitable funding for schools and educational institutions. This includes addressing disparities in funding between wealthy and under-resourced schools and providing additional support for schools in low-income communities.

Access to Higher Education: Gates would advocate for policies that increase access to higher education, including expanding financial aid programs, reducing student loan debt, and supporting initiatives that promote college readiness and success.

Healthcare:

Universal Healthcare Coverage: Gates would prioritize expanding access to healthcare for all individuals, ensuring that everyone has access to essential health services regardless of their income or background. This includes supporting universal healthcare coverage and addressing disparities in healthcare access and outcomes.

Addressing Health Disparities: Gates would support initiatives aimed at reducing health disparities among marginalized communities. This includes funding programs that address social determinants of health, improve access to care, and promote health equity.

Promoting Diversity and Inclusion:

Workplace Diversity:

Equal Employment Opportunities: Gates would advocate for policies that promote diversity and inclusion in the workplace, including enforcing equal employment opportunity laws and supporting initiatives that address workplace discrimination and bias.

Diversity in Leadership: Gates would support efforts to increase diversity in leadership positions across various sectors, including government, business, and academia. This includes promoting mentorship programs, leadership development, and policies that support diverse talent pipelines.

Community Empowerment:

Engagement and Participation: Gates would support policies that encourage community engagement and participation in decision-making processes. This includes fostering inclusive practices that ensure marginalized communities have a voice in shaping policies and programs that affect their lives.

Supporting Local Organizations: Gates would advocate for increased funding and support for local organizations that work to advance social justice and equality. This includes providing grants, resources, and partnerships to organizations focused on community development, advocacy, and support services.

Promoting Social Justice Education:

Educational Programs: Gates would support the development and implementation of educational programs focused on social justice, diversity, and inclusion. This includes integrating social justice topics into school curricula, promoting anti-bias training, and supporting educational initiatives that raise awareness about inequality and discrimination.

Public Awareness Campaigns: Gates would advocate for public awareness campaigns that highlight social justice issues and promote understanding and empathy. This includes using media, technology, and community outreach to raise awareness about the challenges faced by marginalized communities and the importance of addressing social inequality.

Bill Gates' stance on social justice and equality reflects a deep commitment to addressing systemic inequalities and supporting marginalized communities. His policies as President would focus on addressing income inequality, expanding affordable housing, and promoting racial, ethnic, and gender equity. Gates would prioritize ensuring equal opportunities in education and healthcare, advocating for diversity and inclusion in the workplace, and supporting community empowerment. By implementing comprehensive policies and fostering public awareness, Gates aims to create a more just and equitable society, where all individuals have the opportunity to thrive and succeed. His leadership would seek to address the root causes of social injustice and build a more inclusive and fair future for all.

Chapter 13: National Security

Gates' Approach to National Security and Defense

Bill Gates' approach to national security and defense would likely be informed by his emphasis on data-driven decision-making, technological innovation, and global collaboration. His perspective on national security would integrate traditional defense strategies with modern approaches to address a wide range of threats in an increasingly complex global landscape.

Technology-Driven Defense:

Cybersecurity: Gates would prioritize strengthening the nation's cybersecurity defenses to protect critical infrastructure, government systems, and private sector assets from cyber threats. This includes investing in advanced cybersecurity technologies, enhancing threat detection and response capabilities, and fostering collaboration between government agencies, private companies, and international partners.

Artificial Intelligence (AI) and Machine Learning: Gates would advocate for the use of AI and machine learning in national security to improve threat analysis, predictive capabilities, and operational efficiency. This includes developing AI-driven tools for intelligence gathering, surveillance, and strategic planning while ensuring ethical use and minimizing risks associated with AI deployment.

Strategic Defense Initiatives:

Modernizing Military Capabilities: Gates would support the modernization of military capabilities to address emerging threats and adapt to changing strategic environments. This includes investing in next-generation technologies such as autonomous systems, advanced weaponry, and cutting-edge surveillance tools.

Space Security: Recognizing the growing importance of space in national security, Gates would advocate for the development of space-based defense systems and the protection of space assets. This includes addressing threats to satellites and other space infrastructure and promoting international cooperation in space security.

Intelligence and Counterterrorism:

Enhanced Intelligence Capabilities: Gates would emphasize the importance of robust intelligence capabilities to identify and mitigate potential threats. This includes investing in advanced intelligence-gathering technologies, improving data integration and analysis, and enhancing collaboration among intelligence agencies.

Counterterrorism Strategies: Gates would support comprehensive counterterrorism strategies that address both domestic and international threats. This includes strengthening counterterrorism partnerships with allies, investing in preventive measures, and addressing the root causes of extremism.

Global Collaboration and Alliances:

Strengthening Alliances: Gates would prioritize strengthening alliances with key international partners to enhance collective security and address global challenges. This includes working with NATO and other defense alliances to ensure a coordinated response to security threats and promote shared interests.

International Cooperation on Security Issues: Gates would advocate for international cooperation on security issues, including efforts to combat global threats such as terrorism, cyberattacks, and pandemics. This includes participating in international forums, agreements, and initiatives aimed at improving global security and stability.

Human Security and Resilience:

Protecting Civil Liberties: Gates would balance national security measures with the protection of civil liberties and human rights. This includes ensuring that security policies do not infringe upon individual freedoms and privacy, and promoting transparency and accountability in security practices.

Building Resilience: Gates would support initiatives to build resilience in communities and critical infrastructure. This includes preparing for and responding to natural disasters, pandemics, and other emergencies, as well as investing in infrastructure improvements to enhance resilience against various threats.

Strategies for Maintaining Safety and Security

Gates' strategies for maintaining national security and defense would encompass a range of approaches designed to address both conventional and unconventional threats. His focus would be on leveraging technology, fostering collaboration, and implementing proactive measures to ensure the safety and security of the nation.

Technology and Innovation:

Investment in Defense Research and Development: Gates would advocate for increased investment in defense research and development to drive innovation and maintain technological superiority. This includes funding research on emerging technologies, developing new defense systems, and exploring novel approaches to security challenges.

Cyber Defense and Resilience: Gates would prioritize enhancing cyber defense capabilities to protect against cyberattacks and improve resilience. This includes developing advanced cybersecurity protocols, conducting regular security assessments, and implementing measures to safeguard critical infrastructure.

Strategic Military Enhancements:

Modernizing Defense Forces: Gates would support initiatives to modernize defense forces and improve readiness. This includes upgrading equipment, enhancing training programs, and adopting new technologies to ensure that military forces are equipped to handle evolving threats.

Strengthening Defense Infrastructure: Gates would advocate for investments in defense infrastructure, including facilities, bases, and logistics systems. This includes ensuring that defense infrastructure is capable of supporting modern operations and adapting to emerging threats.

Intelligence and Surveillance:

Advanced Intelligence Capabilities: Gates would emphasize the need for advanced intelligence capabilities to detect and counter threats. This includes investing in cutting-edge surveillance technologies, improving data analytics, and enhancing coordination among intelligence agencies.

Proactive Threat Detection: Gates would support strategies for proactive threat detection and prevention. This includes using data-driven approaches to identify potential threats, conducting regular security assessments, and implementing measures to mitigate risks.

Global Security Partnerships:

Enhancing Alliances and Partnerships: Gates would prioritize strengthening security partnerships with allied nations and international organizations. This includes collaborating on joint defense initiatives, sharing intelligence, and participating in joint military exercises to enhance collective security.

International Security Cooperation: Gates would advocate for international cooperation on security issues, including efforts to address transnational threats such as terrorism, cybercrime, and climate change. This includes engaging in diplomatic efforts, participating in multilateral forums, and promoting global security initiatives.

Human and Community Security:

Protecting Civil Rights: Gates would ensure that national security measures respect civil rights and freedoms. This includes implementing oversight mechanisms to prevent abuses of power, promoting transparency in security policies, and protecting individual privacy.

Building Community Resilience: Gates would support programs to build community resilience and preparedness. This includes investing in emergency response systems, providing training for first responders, and supporting community-based initiatives to enhance safety and security.

Addressing Emerging Threats:

Climate Change and Security: Gates would recognize the security implications of climate change and advocate for policies that address both environmental and security challenges. This includes preparing for the impacts of climate change on national security, such as increased frequency of natural disasters and resource conflicts.

Pandemics and Biosecurity: Gates would support strategies to address biosecurity threats and pandemics. This includes investing in research on emerging diseases, enhancing surveillance and response capabilities, and fostering international cooperation to manage global health crises.

Bill Gates' approach to national security and defense would integrate technology-driven solutions, strategic enhancements, and global collaboration to address a broad spectrum of threats. His strategies would focus on leveraging advanced technologies, strengthening alliances, and ensuring that national security measures are balanced with the protection of civil liberties.

By prioritizing investment in defense research and development, enhancing cybersecurity, and fostering international cooperation, Gates aims to maintain safety and security while addressing emerging challenges and promoting resilience. His leadership in national security would seek to ensure that the nation remains well-prepared to respond to both conventional and unconventional threats, while also safeguarding fundamental rights and fostering global stability.

Chapter 14: Integrity and Ethics

Gates' Reputation for Integrity and Ethical Leadership

Bill Gates has long been recognized for his commitment to integrity and ethical leadership, both in his role as a technology pioneer and through his philanthropic efforts. His reputation for these qualities is built on several key aspects of his career and personal values.

Early Career at Microsoft:

Corporate Ethics: During his time at Microsoft, Gates was known for his strong emphasis on ethical business practices and corporate responsibility. While Microsoft faced legal challenges and antitrust issues, Gates worked to address concerns and adapt company practices, demonstrating a commitment to ethical conduct even in complex situations.

Leadership Style: Gates' leadership at Microsoft was characterized by a focus on excellence, accountability, and transparency. His approach to management emphasized the importance of ethical behavior, both within the company and in interactions with competitors and stakeholders.

Philanthropic Efforts:

Transparent Philanthropy: Through the Bill & Melinda Gates Foundation, Gates has exemplified transparency and accountability in philanthropy. The foundation is known for its rigorous evaluation of programs and initiatives, ensuring that resources are used effectively to achieve meaningful outcomes. Gates has championed evidence-based approaches and regularly publishes detailed reports on the foundation's impact and financial practices.

Ethical Giving: Gates has focused on addressing pressing global issues such as health, education, and poverty with a commitment to ethical principles. The foundation's work is guided by a mission to improve lives while adhering to high standards of integrity and respect for those served.

Public Advocacy:

Principled Stance: Gates has consistently taken principled stances on various social, economic, and environmental issues. His advocacy for climate action, global health, and education reform reflects a commitment to ethical considerations and a desire to make a positive impact on society.

Ethical Responsibility: Gates has used his platform to promote ethical behavior in both business and philanthropy. He has spoken out on issues such as corporate social responsibility and the need for businesses to contribute positively to society.

Personal Values:

Commitment to Learning and Growth: Gates has demonstrated a commitment to personal growth and learning, which is integral to ethical leadership. His willingness to adapt, listen to feedback, and engage with diverse perspectives reflects a dedication to ethical principles and continuous improvement.

Focus on Long-Term Impact: Gates' long-term vision for improving global well-being and addressing complex challenges underscores his commitment to ethical decision-making. His approach prioritizes sustainable solutions and long-lasting positive outcomes, aligning with his values of integrity and responsibility.

How These Qualities Would Shape His Presidency

If Bill Gates were to become President, his reputation for integrity and ethical leadership would likely have a profound impact on his approach to governance and policy-making. These qualities would shape his presidency in several key ways:

Ethical Governance:

Transparent Decision-Making: Gates would prioritize transparency in government operations and decision-making processes. This includes providing clear explanations for policy decisions, ensuring that government actions are subject to public scrutiny, and fostering a culture of openness and accountability.

Integrity in Public Office: Gates' commitment to ethical behavior would guide his actions and decisions as President. He would adhere to high standards of integrity, avoiding conflicts of interest and ensuring that personal or financial interests do not influence policy decisions.

Accountability and Oversight:

Strengthening Oversight Mechanisms: Gates would support robust oversight mechanisms to ensure accountability in government and public institutions. This includes enhancing the role of independent watchdogs, promoting transparency in government spending, and addressing instances of corruption or misconduct.

Ethical Standards for Officials: Gates would advocate for high ethical standards for government officials and employees. This includes enforcing codes of conduct, implementing ethics training programs, and taking action against violations of ethical standards.

Evidence-Based Policy:

Data-Driven Decision-Making: Gates' emphasis on evidence-based approaches would inform his policy decisions. He would prioritize data-driven analysis, rigorous evaluation, and empirical research in developing and implementing policies. This approach would ensure that policies are effective, efficient, and aligned with ethical considerations.

Prioritizing Impact: Gates would focus on policies that achieve meaningful and positive outcomes for society. This includes setting clear goals, measuring progress, and making adjustments based on evidence of what works.

Public Trust and Engagement:

Building Trust: Gates' reputation for integrity would help build public trust in government. By demonstrating a commitment to ethical leadership and transparent governance, he would work to restore confidence in public institutions and encourage civic engagement.

Inclusive Decision-Making: Gates would promote inclusive decision-making processes that involve diverse perspectives and stakeholders. This includes engaging with communities, soliciting input from experts, and ensuring that policies reflect the needs and values of all citizens.

Ethical Policy Focus:

Human Rights and Equity: Gates would prioritize policies that promote human rights and social equity. This includes advocating for measures that address systemic inequalities, protect civil liberties, and support marginalized communities.

Environmental Responsibility: Gates' commitment to ethical principles would guide his approach to environmental policies. He would advocate for sustainable practices, address climate change, and ensure that environmental policies are aligned with long-term well-being and ethical considerations.

Corporate and Philanthropic Responsibility:

Ethical Business Practices: Gates would promote ethical practices in both the public and private sectors. This includes advocating for corporate social responsibility, fair business practices, and transparency in corporate governance.

Supporting Effective Philanthropy: Gates would support efforts to improve the effectiveness and accountability of philanthropy. This includes encouraging evidence-based approaches to charitable giving, fostering partnerships between the public and private sectors, and promoting ethical standards in philanthropic endeavors.

Leadership and Role Modeling:

Leading by Example: Gates' personal values of integrity and ethical leadership would serve as a model for others in government and beyond. His approach would inspire a culture of ethical behavior and responsibility, setting a standard for future leaders and policymakers.

Fostering Ethical Culture: Gates would work to cultivate an ethical culture within government and public institutions. This includes promoting values of honesty, fairness, and accountability, and addressing any behaviors or practices that undermine ethical standards.

Bill Gates' reputation for integrity and ethical leadership would significantly influence his presidency, shaping his approach to governance, policy-making, and public engagement. His commitment to transparency, accountability, and evidence-based decision-making would guide his actions and decisions, fostering trust and confidence in government.

By prioritizing ethical principles, promoting inclusivity, and leading by example, Gates would aim to create a presidency marked by high standards of integrity and a focus on achieving positive outcomes for society. His leadership would seek to address complex challenges with a commitment to ethical values and a dedication to the long-term well-being of all citizens.

Chapter 15: Problem-Solving Skills

Gates' Problem-Solving Approach

Bill Gates is renowned for his exceptional problem-solving skills, which have been pivotal in his success as a technology innovator and philanthropist. His approach to problem-solving combines analytical thinking, strategic planning, and collaborative efforts. The following key aspects characterize Gates' problem-solving approach:

Analytical Thinking:

Data-Driven Decisions: Gates relies heavily on data to inform his decisions. He emphasizes the importance of collecting and analyzing relevant data to understand the nature of a problem, identify root causes, and evaluate potential solutions. This analytical approach helps ensure that decisions are based on empirical evidence rather than assumptions.

Systematic Analysis: Gates applies systematic analysis to break down complex problems into manageable components. This involves identifying key variables, understanding relationships between them, and exploring different scenarios to assess potential outcomes.

Strategic Planning:

Goal Setting: Gates focuses on setting clear, measurable goals as a foundation for problem-solving. He believes in defining specific objectives and desired outcomes to guide efforts and measure progress. This approach helps maintain focus and direction in addressing complex issues.

Long-Term Vision: Gates' problem-solving strategy includes developing long-term visions and plans. He considers both immediate and future implications of decisions, ensuring that solutions are sustainable and aligned with broader goals.

Collaborative Efforts:

Engaging Experts: Gates values input from experts and stakeholders in addressing complex problems. He seeks out diverse perspectives and expertise to gain a comprehensive understanding of issues and explore innovative solutions. Collaboration with specialists helps identify best practices and potential pitfalls.

Building Partnerships: Gates often collaborates with organizations, governments, and communities to tackle problems. He recognizes the value of leveraging resources, knowledge, and capabilities from various partners to achieve collective impact.

Innovative Solutions:

Encouraging Innovation: Gates encourages creative thinking and innovation as part of problem-solving. He supports exploring new ideas, technologies, and approaches that have the potential to address challenges more effectively. This includes investing in research and development to drive breakthroughs.

Testing and Iteration: Gates values the process of testing and iterating solutions. He believes in piloting initiatives, gathering feedback, and refining approaches based on real-world results. This iterative process helps improve solutions and adapt to changing conditions.

Focus on Results:

Measuring Impact: Gates emphasizes the importance of measuring and evaluating the impact of solutions. He uses metrics and performance indicators to assess progress, identify areas for improvement, and ensure that solutions achieve their intended outcomes.

Accountability: Gates holds himself and his teams accountable for results. He believes in tracking performance, addressing challenges proactively, and making necessary adjustments to stay on track toward achieving goals.

How Bill Gates Would Tackle Complex National Issues

If Bill Gates were President, his problem-solving skills would influence his approach to addressing complex national issues. His methodology would likely involve a combination of data-driven analysis, strategic planning, collaboration, innovation, and results-focused strategies. Here's how Gates would tackle various national challenges:

Economic Challenges:

Economic Analysis: Gates would start by analyzing economic data to understand the underlying issues, such as unemployment rates, income inequality, and economic growth trends. He would use this analysis to identify key areas of concern and opportunities for intervention.

Strategic Economic Policies: Gates would develop strategic policies aimed at stimulating economic growth, reducing inequality, and creating jobs. This could include investing in infrastructure, supporting small businesses, and implementing tax reforms.

Innovation and Entrepreneurship: Gates would promote innovation and entrepreneurship as drivers of economic progress. He would support initiatives to foster startups, invest in research and development, and create an environment conducive to technological advancement.

Healthcare System Reform:

Data-Driven Healthcare Solutions: Gates would utilize data to assess the performance of the healthcare system, including access to care, health outcomes, and cost efficiency. He would analyze this data to identify gaps and areas for improvement.

Comprehensive Healthcare Plan: Gates would develop a comprehensive healthcare reform plan that addresses issues such as affordability, access, and quality of care. This plan might include expanding coverage, investing in preventive care, and leveraging technology to improve healthcare delivery.

Collaborative Approach: Gates would work with healthcare providers, policymakers, and experts to implement and refine healthcare reforms. He would seek input from stakeholders to ensure that solutions are effective and equitable.

Education Reform:

Educational Data Analysis: Gates would analyze data on educational outcomes, school performance, and access to education to understand the challenges facing the education system. This data-driven approach would guide the development of targeted reforms.

Evidence-Based Education Policies: Gates would advocate for evidence-based policies to improve educational quality and equity. This could include increasing funding for under-resourced schools, supporting teacher training, and implementing programs that address educational disparities.

Innovative Educational Solutions: Gates would explore innovative approaches to education, such as incorporating technology in the classroom, expanding online learning opportunities, and supporting personalized learning experiences.

Climate Change and Environmental Policies:

Environmental Impact Assessment: Gates would use data to assess the environmental impact of current policies and practices. This includes analyzing data on greenhouse gas emissions, energy consumption, and environmental degradation.

Sustainable Solutions: Gates would develop strategies to address climate change and promote sustainability. This could involve investing in renewable energy, supporting conservation efforts, and implementing policies to reduce carbon emissions.

Global Collaboration: Gates would collaborate with international partners to address global environmental challenges. He would support initiatives to share best practices, promote climate action, and advance global environmental agreements.

National Security:

Threat Assessment: Gates would use intelligence and data to assess national security threats, including cyber threats, terrorism, and geopolitical risks. This analysis would inform the development of strategies to enhance security.

Integrated Security Approach: Gates would implement an integrated approach to national security that combines technological solutions, intelligence, and international collaboration. This includes strengthening cybersecurity defenses, modernizing military capabilities, and fostering global security partnerships.

Resilience and Preparedness: Gates would focus on building resilience and preparedness for various security threats. This includes investing in infrastructure, developing emergency response plans, and promoting community resilience.

Social Justice and Equality:

Data-Driven Equity Analysis: Gates would analyze data on social inequalities, including income disparity, access to services, and discrimination. This data would guide the development of policies aimed at promoting social justice and equality.

Targeted Social Policies: Gates would implement targeted policies to address issues such as racial and gender inequality, economic disparity, and access to education and healthcare. These policies would be designed to create a more equitable society.

Community Engagement: Gates would engage with communities to understand their needs and perspectives. He would work with local organizations and stakeholders to develop and implement solutions that address social justice issues effectively.

Bill Gates' problem-solving skills are characterized by a data-driven, strategic, and collaborative approach that emphasizes innovation and results. As President, Gates would apply these skills to tackle complex national issues by analyzing data, setting clear goals, and developing comprehensive strategies.

His focus on evidence-based decision-making, collaboration with experts and stakeholders, and commitment to innovation would guide his efforts to address economic challenges, healthcare reform, education improvement, environmental sustainability, national security, and social justice. Gates' approach would aim to develop effective, sustainable solutions that achieve meaningful outcomes and address the pressing challenges facing the nation.

Chapter 16: Collaboration and Team-Building

Gates' Ability to Build and Lead Teams

Bill Gates' success in building and leading teams is a cornerstone of his achievements in both technology and philanthropy. His approach to team-building and collaboration is characterized by several key principles and practices:

Visionary Leadership:

Setting a Clear Vision: Gates is known for his ability to articulate a clear and compelling vision. At Microsoft, he established a vision for the company that focused on innovation and technological advancement. This clear vision helped align team efforts and motivated employees to work towards common goals.

Inspiring Commitment: Gates' leadership style is inspiring and motivating. He fosters a sense of purpose and commitment among team members by communicating the significance of their work and how it contributes to broader objectives.

Empowering Team Members:

Delegation and Trust: Gates trusts his team members to take ownership of their responsibilities. He delegates tasks effectively, allowing team members to leverage their expertise and make decisions within their areas of responsibility. This empowerment enhances team engagement and productivity.

Encouraging Initiative: Gates encourages team members to take initiative and bring forward new ideas. He values creativity and innovation, promoting an environment where team members feel empowered to propose and explore new approaches.

Building Diverse and Skilled Teams:

Recruiting Talent: Gates is adept at recruiting top talent with diverse skills and expertise.

At Microsoft and the Gates Foundation, he assembled teams with a wide range of backgrounds and perspectives, which contributed to the organizations' success.

Fostering Collaboration: Gates emphasizes the importance of collaboration among team members with different skills and experiences. He believes that diverse teams are more effective at solving complex problems and generating innovative solutions.

Promoting Open Communication:

Transparent Communication: Gates values open and transparent communication within teams. He encourages regular dialogue, feedback, and information sharing, which helps build trust and ensures that team members are informed and aligned.

Active Listening: Gates actively listens to team members' ideas, concerns, and feedback. This approach helps him understand different perspectives, address issues, and make informed decisions that reflect the collective input of the team.

Fostering a Collaborative Culture:

Creating a Collaborative Environment: Gates fosters a culture of collaboration by promoting teamwork and encouraging cross-functional interactions. He values cooperation over competition and works to create an environment where team members support each other and work towards shared goals.

Recognizing Contributions: Gates acknowledges and celebrates the contributions of team members. Recognizing achievements and providing positive reinforcement helps build morale and motivates teams to continue working effectively.

How Bill Gates Would Foster Collaboration in Government

If Bill Gates were President, his ability to build and lead teams would significantly influence his approach to fostering collaboration within the government. Here's how he would apply his team-building skills to create a collaborative and effective government environment:

Establishing a Clear Vision for Government:

Articulating Goals: Gates would set a clear vision for his administration, outlining specific goals and priorities. This vision would guide the work of government agencies and ensure that all efforts are aligned with the broader objectives of the administration.

Inspiring Leadership: Gates would inspire and motivate government officials and employees by communicating the importance of their work and its impact on the nation. He would emphasize the significance of collaboration in achieving the administration's goals.

Building and Leading Effective Teams:

Recruiting and Appointing Talent: Gates would focus on recruiting and appointing individuals with the skills, expertise, and dedication needed to drive progress. He would seek out diverse talent and create teams with a range of perspectives and experiences.

Empowering Officials: Gates would delegate responsibilities and empower government officials to take ownership of their roles. By trusting officials to make decisions and contribute to policy development, he would enhance their engagement and effectiveness.

Promoting Interagency Collaboration:

Encouraging Cross-Agency Cooperation: Gates would promote collaboration among different government agencies and departments. He would establish mechanisms for interagency communication, coordination, and joint problem-solving to address complex issues that require a multifaceted approach.

Breaking Down Silos: Gates would work to break down organizational silos and encourage information sharing between agencies. This includes fostering a culture of openness and collaboration to ensure that agencies work together towards common goals.

Fostering a Collaborative Culture:

Creating Collaborative Work Environments: Gates would create work environments that support collaboration and teamwork. This includes designing office spaces that facilitate communication and collaboration, as well as implementing technology solutions that enhance connectivity and information sharing.

Encouraging Teamwork: Gates would encourage teamwork and collaboration across government projects and initiatives. He would promote a culture where team members support each other, share knowledge, and work together to achieve shared objectives.

Enhancing Public-Private Partnerships:

Building Partnerships: Gates would foster strong partnerships between the government and the private sector. He would work to create collaborative opportunities that leverage the expertise and resources of both sectors to address national challenges.

Promoting Innovation: Gates would encourage public-private partnerships that focus on innovation and technological advancement. By collaborating with private companies, startups, and research institutions, he would seek to drive progress and find creative solutions to complex problems.

Engaging with Stakeholders and Communities:

Soliciting Input: Gates would actively engage with stakeholders, including community organizations, advocacy groups, and the public, to gather input and feedback on government policies and initiatives. This collaborative approach would ensure that policies are informed by diverse perspectives and address the needs of various communities.

Building Trust and Transparency: Gates would prioritize transparency and open communication with the public. By keeping citizens informed and involved in decision-making processes, he would build trust and foster a sense of shared responsibility for addressing national issues.

Implementing Collaborative Problem-Solving:

Leveraging Expertise: Gates would leverage the expertise of government officials, experts, and advisors to tackle complex national issues. He would facilitate collaborative problem-solving by bringing together individuals with diverse skills and knowledge to develop and implement solutions.

Encouraging Innovation: Gates would support innovative approaches to problem-solving that involve collaboration across sectors and disciplines. He would promote initiatives that explore new ideas and technologies to address challenges in effective and creative ways.

Measuring and Improving Collaboration:

Assessing Collaboration Effectiveness: Gates would regularly assess the effectiveness of collaborative efforts within the government. This includes evaluating the success of interagency initiatives, public-private partnerships, and stakeholder engagement activities.

Continuous Improvement: Gates would seek feedback and identify opportunities for improving collaboration. He would implement changes based on lessons learned and best practices to enhance the effectiveness of collaborative efforts over time.

Bill Gates' approach to collaboration and team-building is characterized by visionary leadership, empowerment, and a focus on creating a collaborative culture. As President, Gates would apply these principles to foster effective collaboration within the government, promote interagency cooperation, and build strong public-private partnerships.

His emphasis on clear communication, diverse expertise, and innovative problem-solving would help create a government that works cohesively towards shared goals. By prioritizing collaboration and leveraging the strengths of various stakeholders, Gates would aim to address national challenges effectively and drive positive outcomes for the country.

Chapter 17: Public Perception

Public Opinion on Gates as a Potential President

Bill Gates' public perception as a potential president is influenced by various factors, including his career accomplishments, philanthropic work, and personal demeanor. While his leadership and problem-solving skills are widely respected, public opinion on his suitability as a presidential candidate is nuanced and multifaceted.

Positive Perception:

Accomplished Visionary: Gates is recognized as a visionary leader, particularly for his role in transforming the technology industry with Microsoft and his impact through the Bill & Melinda Gates Foundation. His achievements in innovation and philanthropy contribute to a positive perception of his ability to lead and address national issues.

Philanthropic Reputation: Gates' extensive philanthropic efforts have earned him a reputation for compassion and social responsibility. His work in global health, education, and poverty alleviation resonates with many who see him as a person dedicated to improving lives and making a positive impact.

Problem-Solving Expertise: Gates is admired for his analytical approach and problem-solving skills. His success in addressing complex issues through data-driven strategies and innovative solutions contributes to a belief that he could effectively tackle national challenges.

Skepticism and Concerns:

Political Experience: One of the primary concerns regarding Gates' potential presidency is his lack of direct political experience. Critics may question his ability to navigate the complexities of government and political institutions without prior experience in elected office.

Tech Industry Background: Some may view Gates' background in the tech industry with skepticism, particularly if they perceive him as disconnected from the political and social realities faced by average citizens. There may be concerns about whether his tech-oriented approach would translate effectively to broader policy issues.

Philanthropic Focus: While Gates' philanthropic work is widely praised, some critics may question whether his focus on global health and development translates to effective domestic policy. They may be concerned that his priorities might not fully address the needs and concerns of American citizens.

Neutral or Mixed Views:

Unfamiliarity with Policy: For some, Gates' lack of experience in government may result in mixed opinions about his potential effectiveness as president. While his problem-solving skills are acknowledged, there may be uncertainty about how well he would adapt to the political and administrative responsibilities of the presidency.

Public Perception of Wealth: Gates' wealth and status as a billionaire could influence public perception. While some view this as an advantage, believing that his financial resources could support effective governance, others might be concerned about the influence of wealth on his decision-making and priorities.

Strategies for Building Public Support

If Bill Gates were to pursue a presidential candidacy, building public support would be essential. He would need to address concerns, leverage his strengths, and engage with voters effectively. The following strategies could help him build and strengthen public support:

Emphasizing Accomplishments and Vision:

Showcasing Achievements: Gates should highlight his significant accomplishments in technology and philanthropy, emphasizing how these experiences have equipped him with valuable skills for leadership. By showcasing his track record of success, he can build credibility and demonstrate his ability to effect positive change.

Articulating a Clear Vision: Gates would need to articulate a clear and compelling vision for his presidency. This vision should address key national issues, such as economic growth, healthcare reform, and education, and outline specific goals and strategies for achieving them. A strong vision can inspire and attract supporters.

Addressing Concerns About Experience:

Building a Strong Team: Gates could mitigate concerns about his lack of political experience by assembling a diverse and experienced team of advisors and officials. By surrounding himself with experts and seasoned professionals, he can demonstrate his commitment to effective governance and reassure voters of his capability to navigate political challenges.

Engaging in Political Processes: Gates should actively engage in political processes, such as participating in debates, town hall meetings, and policy discussions. This would help him familiarize himself with political dynamics and demonstrate his willingness to engage with the public and address their concerns.

Connecting with Voters:

Personal Outreach: Gates should engage in direct outreach to voters, including attending community events, participating in public forums, and meeting with various stakeholder groups. Personal interactions can help build rapport and trust, allowing Gates to connect with voters on a more personal level.

Listening and Responding: Actively listening to voters' concerns and responding to their feedback is crucial. Gates should demonstrate that he values public input and is committed to addressing the issues that matter most to citizens. This approach can help build credibility and support.

Leveraging Philanthropic Experience:

Highlighting Positive Impact: Gates should emphasize the positive impact of his philanthropic work, showcasing specific examples of successful initiatives and programs. By demonstrating how his efforts have made a difference, he can build support among voters who value social responsibility and effective problem-solving.

Translating Experience to Policy: Gates could articulate how his philanthropic experience has provided him with insights and skills relevant to public policy. He should explain how his approach to addressing global challenges can be adapted to tackle domestic issues effectively.

Building a Broad Coalition:

Engaging Diverse Constituencies: Gates should work to build a broad coalition of supporters by engaging with diverse constituencies, including different demographic groups, political affiliations, and interest areas. Building a diverse base of support can help expand his appeal and increase his chances of winning broad-based support.

Collaborating with Key Influencers: Partnering with influential figures, organizations, and community leaders can help Gates gain endorsements and build credibility. Collaborations with respected voices can enhance his visibility and support among various voter groups.

Communicating Effectively:

Utilizing Media and Technology: Gates should leverage media and technology to communicate his message and engage with voters. This includes using social media platforms, participating in interviews, and utilizing digital tools to reach a wide audience and share his vision and policies.

Crafting a Strong Narrative: Developing a strong narrative that conveys Gates' personal journey, values, and goals can help shape public perception. A compelling narrative can resonate with voters and create a connection between Gates and the electorate.

Demonstrating Commitment to Public Service:

Showcasing Dedication: Gates should demonstrate his commitment to public service by actively engaging in community and public service initiatives. This includes participating in charitable activities, supporting local causes, and showing a genuine dedication to improving the lives of citizens.

Emphasizing Transparency and Accountability: Gates should emphasize his commitment to transparency and accountability in government. By highlighting his dedication to ethical leadership and open communication, he can build trust and support among voters.

Public perception of Bill Gates as a potential president is influenced by his accomplishments, philanthropic work, and the perceived gaps in political experience. To build public support, Gates would need to address concerns, highlight his strengths, and engage with voters effectively. By emphasizing his achievements, articulating a clear vision, addressing experience-related concerns, and connecting with diverse constituencies, Gates can work to build a broad base of support.

Leveraging his philanthropic experience, collaborating with key influencers, and demonstrating a commitment to public service would further enhance his appeal and strengthen his candidacy. Through effective communication and outreach, Gates can address public concerns and build a positive and supportive image as a presidential candidate.

Chapter 18: Overcoming Challenges

Potential Challenges Gates Might Face

As a potential president, Bill Gates would encounter several significant challenges. These obstacles could range from political and public perception issues to practical governance hurdles. Understanding these challenges and developing strategies to address them would be crucial for Gates' success.

Lack of Political Experience:

Challenge: Gates' limited experience in elected office and government administration might be a significant challenge. Voters and critics may question his ability to navigate the complexities of the political landscape and effectively manage a government.

Impact: Lack of political experience could lead to skepticism about his decision-making capabilities, understanding of policy intricacies, and ability to build consensus in a diverse political environment.

Political Resistance:

Challenge: Gates could face resistance from established political figures and institutions, including Congress, political parties, and special interest groups. Political opposition could manifest as legislative gridlock, challenges in passing policies, or attempts to undermine his presidency.

Impact: Political resistance could hinder the implementation of Gates' policies and initiatives, affecting his ability to achieve his goals and fulfill campaign promises.

Public Perception and Trust:

Challenge: Gates may struggle with public perception issues, particularly related to his wealth and background. Critics might view him as disconnected from everyday Americans' concerns or question his motivations and priorities.

Impact: Negative public perception could impact Gates' ability to build broad-based support, garner trust, and effectively communicate his vision and policies.

Navigating Bureaucracy:

Challenge: Managing and reforming a large and complex bureaucracy can be challenging, particularly for someone without extensive government experience. Gates would need to understand and effectively work within the constraints and dynamics of the federal bureaucracy.

Impact: Inefficiencies and resistance within the bureaucracy could impede Gates' efforts to implement reforms and drive government efficiency.

Balancing Diverse Interests:

Challenge: As president, Gates would need to balance the interests of various stakeholders, including political parties, interest groups, and the general public. Achieving consensus and addressing conflicting interests could be a significant challenge.

Impact: Difficulty in balancing diverse interests could result in policy compromises, delayed decision-making, and challenges in achieving legislative goals.

Managing Economic and Social Issues:

Challenge: Gates would face complex economic and social issues, such as income inequality, healthcare reform, and climate change. Addressing these challenges would require effective strategies and solutions that resonate with a broad range of Americans.

Impact: Failure to effectively address these issues could lead to dissatisfaction among voters, decreased support, and challenges in achieving policy objectives.

International Relations:

Challenge: Navigating international relations and addressing global challenges would be another significant challenge. Gates would need to manage diplomatic relationships, trade agreements, and international collaborations effectively.

Impact: Poor handling of international relations could affect the U.S.'s global standing, impact trade and security interests, and create diplomatic tensions.

How Bill Gates Would Address and Overcome These Obstacles

To overcome these challenges, Bill Gates would need to employ a range of strategies, leveraging his skills, experience, and resources effectively. Here's how he could address and overcome these obstacles:

Addressing Lack of Political Experience:

Building a Strong Team: Gates should assemble a team of experienced advisors and officials with deep knowledge of government operations and policy. This team would provide expertise, guidance, and support in navigating political complexities.

Engaging in Political Processes: Actively participating in political processes, such as working with Congress, engaging in bipartisan discussions, and understanding legislative procedures, would help Gates adapt to the political environment and build effective working relationships.

Managing Political Resistance:

Building Consensus: Gates should focus on building bipartisan support for his policies and initiatives. By engaging with members of both parties, addressing their concerns, and seeking common ground, he can overcome resistance and achieve legislative goals.

Effective Communication: Clear and transparent communication about his policies, goals, and motivations can help address resistance and build understanding. Gates should use public speeches, media appearances, and direct outreach to convey his vision and foster support.

Improving Public Perception and Trust:

Engaging with the Public: Gates should actively engage with the public through town hall meetings, listening tours, and community events. By addressing concerns, listening to feedback, and demonstrating empathy, he can build trust and improve his public image.

Showcasing Relatable Initiatives: Gates could focus on initiatives and policies that directly impact and benefit everyday Americans. By highlighting his commitment to addressing issues that matter to citizens, he can improve his relatability and credibility.

Navigating Bureaucracy:

Streamlining Processes: Gates should work to streamline bureaucratic processes and improve government efficiency. This includes implementing technology solutions, reducing red tape, and fostering a culture of innovation within government agencies.

Fostering Collaboration: Building collaborative relationships with key bureaucratic leaders and stakeholders can help Gates navigate the complexities of the bureaucracy and facilitate the implementation of reforms.

Balancing Diverse Interests:

Engaging Stakeholders: Gates should actively engage with a broad range of stakeholders, including political leaders, interest groups, and community organizations. By understanding their perspectives and finding common ground, he can effectively balance diverse interests and achieve policy objectives.

Compromising and Negotiating: Gates would need to be skilled in negotiating and compromising to address conflicting interests. By seeking mutually beneficial solutions and fostering a collaborative approach, he can achieve balanced outcomes.

Managing Economic and Social Issues:

Developing Evidence-Based Policies: Gates should rely on data-driven, evidence-based policies to address economic and social challenges. By using empirical data and expert analysis, he can develop effective strategies that resonate with a broad range of Americans.

Implementing Pilot Programs: Testing and piloting new initiatives on a smaller scale before full implementation can help identify potential issues and refine strategies. This approach allows Gates to address challenges and make necessary adjustments based on real-world feedback.

Navigating International Relations:

Building Strong Diplomatic Relationships: Gates should prioritize building strong relationships with international leaders and engaging in diplomatic efforts. By fostering cooperation and collaboration, he can effectively address global challenges and enhance the U.S.'s global standing.

Balancing Domestic and International Priorities: Gates should work to balance domestic and international priorities, ensuring that U.S. interests are well-represented while contributing to global solutions. This includes managing trade agreements, security partnerships, and environmental initiatives.

Bill Gates would face several challenges as a potential president, including his lack of political experience, political resistance, public perception issues, and complex governance and international relations. To overcome these obstacles, Gates would need to leverage his strengths, including his problem-solving skills, visionary leadership, and commitment to innovation.

By building a strong team, engaging with the public, managing bureaucracy, balancing diverse interests, and addressing economic and social issues effectively, Gates can work to navigate and overcome these challenges. His ability to adapt, collaborate, and communicate effectively would be key to his success in addressing the complex issues of the presidency and achieving his goals for the nation.

Chapter 19: Campaign Strategy

Outline of Gates' Campaign Strategy

Bill Gates' campaign strategy for a presidential run would need to be comprehensive and well-coordinated, reflecting his unique strengths and addressing potential challenges. A successful campaign strategy would encompass several key components, including message development, voter outreach, fundraising, and media engagement. Here's a detailed outline of how Gates might approach his campaign:

Message Development:

Defining Key Messages: Gates would need to develop clear and compelling key messages that resonate with voters. These messages should emphasize his vision for America, his accomplishments, and his plans for addressing national issues.

Crafting a Narrative: A strong campaign narrative would be essential for connecting with voters. Gates should develop a narrative that highlights his personal journey, achievements, and the values that drive his vision for the country.

Tailoring Messages: Messages should be tailored to different voter demographics and regions, addressing specific concerns and priorities relevant to various groups.

Voter Outreach:

Targeting Key Demographics: Gates should identify and target key voter demographics, including independents, moderates, and swing voters. He would need to tailor outreach efforts to address the concerns and interests of these groups.

Grassroots Engagement: Building a grassroots network of supporters and volunteers would be crucial. Gates should engage in grassroots campaigning through local events, town hall meetings, and community outreach.

Digital Outreach: Leveraging digital platforms, including social media, email campaigns, and online advertising, would be essential for reaching a broad audience. Gates should use these tools to communicate directly with voters, share his message, and mobilize support.

Fundraising:

Developing a Fundraising Plan: Gates would need a robust fundraising strategy to support his campaign. This includes soliciting contributions from individual donors, political action committees (PACs), and potentially leveraging his own resources.

Organizing Fundraising Events: Hosting fundraising events, both in-person and virtual, would help generate financial support and build relationships with donors. Gates should focus on high-profile events and outreach to influential donors.

Utilizing Digital Fundraising: Implementing digital fundraising techniques, such as online donation platforms and crowdfunding, would allow Gates to engage with small-dollar donors and build a broad base of financial support.

Media Engagement:

Media Relations: Building strong relationships with media outlets and journalists would be crucial for securing positive coverage and managing public perception. Gates should engage in interviews, press conferences, and media events to communicate his message.

Campaign Advertising: Developing and airing campaign ads across television, radio, and digital platforms would help raise visibility and promote key messages. Gates should focus on creating impactful ads that highlight his strengths and contrast his vision with opponents.

Managing Media Coverage: Effectively managing media coverage, including addressing negative stories and controlling the narrative, would be important for maintaining a positive public image.

Debate and Public Speaking:

Preparing for Debates: Gates should prepare thoroughly for presidential debates by researching opponent positions, practicing responses, and developing strong arguments. Successful debate performances would be critical for showcasing his qualifications and vision.

Engaging in Public Speaking: Gates should engage in public speaking opportunities to address various audiences, including policy forums, community events, and academic institutions. Effective public speaking would help articulate his vision and build rapport with voters.

Coalition Building:

Forming Alliances: Building alliances with key political figures, organizations, and community leaders would help strengthen Gates' support base. Endorsements from influential individuals and groups can lend credibility and increase his appeal.

Uniting Diverse Groups: Gates should work to build a broad coalition that includes diverse voter groups, including progressives, moderates, and independents. Uniting these groups around common goals and values would be essential for winning broad-based support.

Field Operations:

Organizing Campaign Teams: Establishing a well-organized campaign team with roles focused on field operations, data analysis, and voter outreach would be crucial for effective campaign management.

Mobilizing Volunteers: Recruiting and training volunteers for canvassing, phone banking, and voter registration efforts would help increase grassroots support and engagement.

Polling and Data Analysis:

Conducting Polling: Regularly conducting polls and surveys would provide insights into voter attitudes, preferences, and concerns. This data would help refine campaign strategies and messages.

Analyzing Data: Utilizing data analytics to track campaign performance, voter engagement, and demographic trends would allow Gates to make informed decisions and adjust strategies as needed.

Key Messages and Themes

For a presidential campaign, Gates would need to craft key messages and themes that effectively convey his vision, accomplishments, and plans. Here are some potential key messages and themes for Gates' campaign:

Vision for Innovation and Progress:

Message: "A Future Built on Innovation" – Gates would emphasize his commitment to driving technological advancement and innovation to address national challenges and create new opportunities.

Theme: Highlighting his experience in technology and philanthropy, Gates would present a vision of a forward-looking America where innovation drives economic growth, improves quality of life, and addresses critical issues like health care and education.

Commitment to Global Leadership:

Message: "Leading with Purpose" – Gates would focus on his experience in global health and development, positioning himself as a leader with the ability to address international challenges and strengthen the U.S.'s role on the global stage.

Theme: Emphasizing his track record of impactful global work, Gates would advocate for a strong and responsible U.S. presence in international affairs, promoting diplomacy, collaboration, and global problem-solving.

Focus on Effective Problem-Solving:

Message: "Solving Problems, Making a Difference" – Gates would highlight his problem-solving skills and data-driven approach to addressing complex issues. He would stress his ability to find effective solutions and make a tangible impact on key national challenges.

Theme: Presenting himself as a pragmatic and results-oriented leader, Gates would appeal to voters who value practical solutions and evidence-based decision-making.

Dedication to Social Responsibility:

Message: "Building a Fairer, More Equitable Society" – Gates would emphasize his commitment to social justice, equality, and addressing systemic issues. He would advocate for policies that promote economic fairness, social equity, and opportunity for all.

Theme: Drawing on his philanthropic work, Gates would promote a vision of a more inclusive and compassionate America where everyone has the opportunity to succeed and thrive.

Commitment to Climate Action:

Message: "Leading the Way in Climate Solutions" – Gates would focus on his dedication to addressing climate change and promoting sustainable energy. He would advocate for bold climate policies and innovative solutions to protect the environment and combat global warming.

Theme: Emphasizing his work on climate issues, Gates would present himself as a leader committed to environmental stewardship and long-term sustainability.

Strengthening Education and Healthcare:

Message: "Investing in Our Future" – Gates would highlight his commitment to improving education and healthcare systems. He would advocate for policies that enhance access to quality education and healthcare, fostering a healthier and more educated population.

Theme: Building on his philanthropic contributions to education and health, Gates would present a vision of investing in critical sectors to ensure that all Americans have access to the resources they need to succeed.

Promoting Economic Growth and Innovation:

Message: "Creating Jobs, Driving Economic Growth" – Gates would focus on his plans for economic development and job creation, emphasizing his commitment to fostering innovation, supporting entrepreneurship, and driving economic progress.

Theme: Gates would advocate for policies that stimulate economic growth, support businesses, and create opportunities for workers, positioning himself as a champion of economic advancement.

Ensuring Effective Governance:

Message: "A Government That Works for You" – Gates would stress his commitment to efficient and transparent governance. He would advocate for reforms that improve government operations, reduce bureaucracy, and enhance accountability.

Theme: Emphasizing his experience in problem-solving and innovation, Gates would present himself as a leader capable of driving effective and efficient governance that serves the needs of the American people.

Bill Gates' campaign strategy would need to be multifaceted, incorporating message development, voter outreach, fundraising, and media engagement. By crafting compelling key messages and themes, Gates can effectively communicate his vision, accomplishments, and plans to voters. Addressing challenges related to political experience, public perception, and campaign management would be essential for building support and achieving electoral success. Through a well-coordinated campaign strategy and a focus on key messages that resonate with voters, Gates can position himself as a strong and effective candidate for the presidency.

Chapter 20: Building a Winning Coalition

Strategies for Building a Diverse and Inclusive Coalition

Building a diverse and inclusive coalition is crucial for any successful presidential campaign. For Bill Gates, this means assembling a broad base of support that spans across different demographics, political affiliations, and interest groups. To achieve this, Gates would need to employ several strategies that emphasize inclusion, collaboration, and outreach. Here's a detailed look at how Gates might approach building a winning coalition:

Identifying Key Demographics:

Assessing Voter Segments: Gates would need to identify and understand various key voter demographics, including young voters, minorities, women, seniors, working-class voters, and independents. Each group has unique concerns and priorities that Gates would need to address.

Analyzing Voting Trends: Utilizing data analytics to study voting patterns and trends can provide insights into which demographics are pivotal for gaining electoral success and how best to engage them.

Crafting Inclusive Messaging:

Developing Tailored Messages: Gates should create tailored messages that resonate with different demographic groups. For instance, focusing on educational reform for younger voters, healthcare for seniors, and economic opportunities for working-class voters.

Promoting Shared Values: Emphasizing shared values such as equality, innovation, and community can help bridge gaps between diverse groups. Gates should highlight common goals and how his vision aligns with the aspirations of various voter segments.

Engaging Community Leaders and Influencers:

Building Alliances: Partnering with respected community leaders, activists, and influencers can help Gates gain credibility and reach diverse groups. These alliances can provide valuable endorsements and amplify his message within various communities.

Hosting Community Events: Organizing events with community leaders and engaging directly with local organizations can strengthen connections with different voter groups and demonstrate Gates' commitment to addressing their specific needs.

Fostering Grassroots Support:

Mobilizing Volunteers: Recruiting and training a diverse group of volunteers to support campaign activities such as canvassing, phone banking, and voter registration drives can help expand outreach efforts.

Encouraging Local Involvement: Encouraging local involvement and leadership in grassroots efforts can foster a sense of ownership and investment in the campaign, leading to stronger grassroots support and outreach.

Addressing Specific Concerns:

Understanding Unique Issues: Gates should make a concerted effort to understand and address the unique concerns of different demographic groups. For instance, addressing issues related to racial justice, economic inequality, or environmental justice can help build trust and support among targeted groups.

Offering Solutions: Providing concrete solutions and policy proposals that directly address the concerns of different demographics can enhance Gates' appeal and demonstrate his commitment to addressing their needs.

Utilizing Digital Tools:

Social Media Campaigns: Leveraging social media platforms to reach and engage with diverse voter groups can help amplify Gates' message and build a broad base of support. Tailoring content to different platforms and audiences can enhance outreach and engagement.

Targeted Advertising: Using data-driven advertising to target specific demographics with customized messages can increase the effectiveness of outreach efforts and ensure that Gates' campaign resonates with various voter segments.

Building a Broad Coalition of Endorsements:

Seeking Diverse Endorsements: Securing endorsements from a wide range of political figures, organizations, and community leaders can help build a broad coalition of support. These endorsements can lend credibility and attract voters who respect the endorsers.

Highlighting Cross-Party Support: Demonstrating support from across the political spectrum can help appeal to independents and moderate voters, showcasing Gates' ability to bridge political divides and build a unified coalition.

Promoting Inclusivity in Campaign Activities:

Ensuring Diverse Representation: Ensuring diverse representation within the campaign team and leadership can help build credibility and resonate with various voter groups. A diverse team reflects a commitment to inclusivity and understanding of different perspectives.

Creating Accessible Campaign Platforms: Making campaign events, materials, and communications accessible to people with disabilities and language barriers can enhance inclusivity and reach a broader audience.

Engaging Various Voter Demographics

To effectively engage various voter demographics, Gates would need to tailor his approach to meet the specific needs and interests of each group. Here's a breakdown of how he might engage key demographics:

Young Voters:

Focus on Education and Innovation: Gates should emphasize his plans for education reform and technological innovation, which are likely to resonate with younger voters. Highlighting initiatives that support STEM education and job creation in tech sectors can appeal to this group.

Leveraging Social Media: Engaging with young voters through social media platforms and online communities can help Gates connect with this demographic. Creating engaging content and participating in online discussions can enhance outreach.

Minority Communities:

Addressing Racial and Social Justice: Gates should address issues related to racial and social justice, including police reform, economic disparities, and voting rights. Demonstrating a commitment to addressing these concerns can build trust and support within minority communities.

Partnering with Advocacy Groups: Collaborating with advocacy organizations that focus on minority rights and issues can help Gates gain support and credibility within these communities.

Women Voters:

Promoting Gender Equality: Gates should emphasize policies that promote gender equality, such as equal pay, reproductive rights, and family leave. Highlighting his commitment to addressing gender-specific issues can resonate with women voters.

Engaging with Women's Organizations: Building relationships with women's advocacy groups and participating in events focused on women's issues can enhance Gates' appeal among female voters.

Seniors:

Focus on Healthcare and Social Security: Gates should prioritize discussions around healthcare reform, Social Security, and other issues important to seniors. Demonstrating a commitment to improving healthcare access and financial security for older Americans can build support.

Participating in Senior-Centric Events: Engaging with senior organizations and participating in events focused on issues affecting older Americans can help Gates connect with this demographic.

Working-Class Voters:

Addressing Economic Concerns: Gates should focus on economic policies that address job creation, wage growth, and economic opportunity for working-class voters. Highlighting plans to support small businesses and improve labor conditions can resonate with this group.

Engaging in Community Outreach: Participating in community events and listening to the concerns of working-class voters can help Gates build rapport and demonstrate his commitment to addressing their needs.

Independent and Swing Voters:

Presenting a Unifying Vision: Gates should emphasize his ability to bridge political divides and present a unifying vision that appeals to independents and swing voters. Highlighting bipartisan support and collaborative approaches can enhance his appeal.

Focusing on Pragmatic Solutions: Offering pragmatic, evidence-based solutions to key issues can attract independents and swing voters who prioritize effective governance over partisan politics.

Building a winning coalition requires a strategic approach that emphasizes diversity, inclusion, and targeted engagement. For Bill Gates, this means crafting tailored messages for different demographics, fostering grassroots support, and leveraging digital tools to reach a broad audience. By addressing the unique concerns of various voter groups and promoting shared values, Gates can build a diverse coalition that supports his vision and enhances his chances of electoral success. Engaging with community leaders, forming alliances, and ensuring inclusivity in campaign activities will further strengthen his coalition and drive a successful campaign.

Chapter 21: A Vision for the Future

Gates' Vision for America in 2028 and Beyond

Bill Gates' vision for America in 2028 and beyond reflects his longstanding commitment to innovation, problem-solving, and global leadership. His presidency would be guided by a forward-thinking approach, aiming to address the pressing challenges of the present while preparing the nation for future opportunities. Gates' vision encompasses several key areas, including technological advancement, economic growth, education reform, healthcare innovation, and global engagement.

Technological Advancement and Innovation:

Driving Technological Progress: Gates envisions America as a global leader in technological innovation. His presidency would prioritize investments in emerging technologies such as artificial intelligence, quantum computing, and renewable energy. By fostering an environment conducive to technological advancements, Gates aims to position the U.S. at the forefront of the next technological revolution.

Promoting Digital Infrastructure: Enhancing digital infrastructure, including expanding high-speed internet access and improving cybersecurity, would be central to Gates' vision. Ensuring that all Americans have access to reliable internet and protecting digital assets from cyber threats would support economic growth and innovation.

Economic Growth and Job Creation:

Fostering Economic Innovation: Gates would focus on creating a robust and resilient economy by supporting innovation and entrepreneurship. Policies to promote research and development, support startups, and incentivize private investment in technology and infrastructure would drive economic growth.

Addressing Income Inequality: Tackling income inequality would be a priority. Gates would advocate for policies that provide opportunities for all Americans, including workforce training programs, improved access to education, and targeted economic assistance for underserved communities.

Education Reform:

Enhancing Education Systems: Gates' vision includes a comprehensive overhaul of the education system to ensure that it meets the needs of the 21st century. This would involve integrating technology into classrooms, supporting personalized learning, and emphasizing STEM education to prepare students for future careers.

Expanding Access to Quality Education: Gates would work to ensure that high-quality education is accessible to all students, regardless of their geographic location or socioeconomic status. This includes investing in public schools, providing support for underserved communities, and promoting educational equity.

Healthcare Innovation and Reform:

Advancing Healthcare Technologies: Gates' focus on healthcare would involve leveraging technology to improve health outcomes and reduce costs. This includes supporting advancements in telemedicine, personalized medicine, and health data analytics to enhance the quality of care.

Reforming the Healthcare System: Gates would advocate for comprehensive healthcare reform aimed at expanding access to affordable care, improving the efficiency of healthcare delivery, and addressing disparities in health outcomes across different populations.

Climate Action and Sustainability:

Addressing Climate Change: A key component of Gates' vision is addressing climate change through ambitious policies and initiatives. His presidency would prioritize investments in clean energy technologies, such as advanced solar and wind power, and support for research into new methods of reducing greenhouse gas emissions.

Promoting Environmental Sustainability: Gates would champion policies that promote environmental sustainability, including conservation efforts, sustainable agriculture practices, and initiatives to protect natural resources and biodiversity.

Global Engagement and Leadership:

Strengthening Global Alliances: Gates envisions the U.S. playing a leading role in global affairs by strengthening alliances and partnerships. His presidency would focus on promoting international cooperation on issues such as climate change, global health, and security.

Supporting Global Development: Gates' experience with global health and development would inform his approach to supporting international development efforts. His presidency would continue to support initiatives aimed at improving health, education, and economic opportunities in developing countries.

How His Presidency Could Shape the Future

Bill Gates' presidency has the potential to significantly shape the future of America and the world through transformative policies and innovative approaches. Here's how his leadership could influence various aspects of American life and global affairs:

Transforming the Economy:

Driving Innovation: By prioritizing technological advancements and supporting research and development, Gates' presidency could lead to the creation of new industries, job opportunities, and economic growth. This focus on innovation would help ensure that the U.S. remains competitive in a rapidly changing global economy.

Reducing Inequality: Gates' efforts to address income inequality and provide economic opportunities for underserved communities could result in a more equitable and inclusive economy. His policies could help reduce poverty, improve living standards, and promote social mobility.

Revolutionizing Education:

Preparing Future Generations: Gates' education reforms could lead to a more dynamic and effective education system that prepares students for the challenges of the future. By integrating technology and emphasizing STEM education, Gates could help cultivate a generation of skilled and innovative leaders.

Promoting Educational Equity: Expanding access to quality education and addressing disparities could improve educational outcomes for students from all backgrounds. Gates' focus on equity could help ensure that every student has the opportunity to succeed and contribute to a more knowledgeable and skilled workforce.

Advancing Healthcare:

Improving Health Outcomes: Gates' focus on healthcare innovation and reform could lead to significant improvements in health outcomes and a more efficient healthcare system. By leveraging technology and advancing medical research, his presidency could enhance the quality of care and reduce healthcare costs.

Expanding Access: Efforts to expand access to affordable healthcare could address disparities and ensure that all Americans receive the care they need. Gates' policies could help improve health equity and address systemic issues within the healthcare system.

Addressing Climate Change:

Leading on Climate Action: Gates' commitment to climate action could position the U.S. as a global leader in addressing climate change. His policies could drive significant progress in reducing greenhouse gas emissions, advancing clean energy technologies, and promoting environmental sustainability.

Inspiring Global Action: By demonstrating leadership on climate issues, Gates could inspire other nations to take action and collaborate on global efforts to combat climate change. His presidency could contribute to international agreements and initiatives aimed at protecting the environment.

Enhancing Global Influence:

Promoting International Cooperation: Gates' approach to global engagement and diplomacy could strengthen international alliances and foster greater cooperation on global challenges. His presidency could enhance the U.S.'s role in addressing issues such as global health, security, and economic development.

Supporting Global Development: Continued support for international development efforts could improve conditions in developing countries and contribute to global stability and prosperity. Gates' experience and leadership could drive positive change in global health, education, and economic opportunities.

Bill Gates' vision for America in 2028 and beyond is characterized by a commitment to technological innovation, economic growth, education reform, healthcare advancement, climate action, and global leadership. His presidency could significantly shape the future by addressing critical challenges, promoting inclusivity, and driving progress across various sectors. Through transformative policies and a forward-thinking approach, Gates has the potential to create a more equitable, innovative, and sustainable future for America and the world. His leadership could not only address immediate concerns but also lay the foundation for long-term success and global impact.

Chapter 22: The Legacy of Bill Gates

Potential Legacy of Gates as President

The potential legacy of Bill Gates as president would be shaped by his unique combination of experience in technology, philanthropy, and global leadership. Gates' tenure could leave a lasting impact on various aspects of American society and the global community. His legacy would likely be defined by transformative policies, innovative approaches, and a commitment to addressing some of the world's most pressing challenges. Here's a detailed exploration of what Gates' presidential legacy might entail:

Technological Advancement and Innovation:

Driving Technological Progress: Gates' focus on technological innovation could lead to significant advancements in fields such as artificial intelligence, quantum computing, and clean energy. His presidency might be remembered for fostering an environment that nurtures cutting-edge research and development, positioning the U.S. as a global leader in technology.

Strengthening Digital Infrastructure: By investing in digital infrastructure and improving cybersecurity, Gates could enhance the nation's technological capabilities and resilience. His efforts to expand high-speed internet access and modernize digital systems would likely be seen as crucial steps in preparing America for a digital future.

Economic Growth and Inclusivity:

Boosting Economic Innovation: Gates' emphasis on innovation and entrepreneurship could lead to the creation of new industries and job opportunities. His legacy could include a revitalized economy driven by technological advancements and a robust support system for startups and small businesses.

Addressing Income Inequality: Through policies aimed at reducing income inequality and providing opportunities for underserved communities, Gates could contribute to a more equitable and inclusive economy. His legacy might include progress in addressing economic disparities and enhancing social mobility.

Education Reform and Empowerment:

Transforming Education Systems: Gates' efforts to reform education could leave a lasting impact on how students are prepared for the future. By integrating technology into classrooms, supporting personalized learning, and expanding access to quality education, his presidency could be remembered for modernizing education and fostering a skilled workforce.

Promoting Educational Equity: Gates' focus on educational equity and access could result in significant improvements in educational outcomes for students from diverse backgrounds. His legacy might include progress in closing educational gaps and ensuring that every student has the opportunity to succeed.

Healthcare Innovation and Access:

Advancing Healthcare Technologies: Gates' emphasis on healthcare innovation could lead to breakthroughs in medical technology, telemedicine, and personalized medicine. His presidency might be remembered for advancing health outcomes and reducing healthcare costs through technological advancements.

Expanding Access to Care: His efforts to reform the healthcare system and expand access to affordable care could address disparities and improve health equity. Gates' legacy could include progress in making healthcare more accessible and efficient for all Americans.

Climate Action and Environmental Stewardship:

Leading on Climate Change: Gates' commitment to addressing climate change could position the U.S. as a global leader in environmental sustainability. His presidency might be remembered for implementing ambitious climate policies, investing in clean energy, and promoting sustainability.

Inspiring Global Action: By taking a strong stance on climate issues, Gates could inspire other nations to follow suit and collaborate on global environmental initiatives. His legacy might include a significant contribution to international efforts to combat climate change and protect natural resources.

Global Leadership and Development:

Strengthening International Alliances: Gates' approach to global engagement could enhance the U.S.'s role in international affairs. His presidency might be remembered for building strong alliances, promoting diplomacy, and addressing global challenges through collaboration.

Supporting Global Development: Gates' experience in global health and development could lead to continued support for international development efforts. His legacy might include progress in improving health, education, and economic opportunities in developing countries.

Ethical Leadership and Integrity:

Championing Ethical Governance: Gates' reputation for integrity and ethical leadership could set a high standard for governance. His presidency might be remembered for promoting transparency, accountability, and ethical practices in government.

Promoting Public Trust: By upholding strong ethical standards and demonstrating a commitment to public service, Gates could contribute to restoring and enhancing public trust in government institutions.

Long-Term Impact on the Country and the World

Bill Gates' presidency could have a profound long-term impact on both the United States and the global community. Here's a detailed look at the potential long-term effects of his leadership:

Economic Transformation:

Innovation-Driven Economy: Gates' focus on technological innovation and entrepreneurship could lead to a more dynamic and competitive economy. The long-term impact might include sustained economic growth driven by advancements in technology and new industries.

Inclusive Economic Policies: By addressing income inequality and expanding economic opportunities, Gates' presidency could contribute to a more equitable society. The long-term impact might include reduced economic disparities and improved social mobility.

Educational Advancement:

Future-Ready Workforce: Gates' education reforms could result in a workforce that is better prepared for the challenges of the future. The long-term impact might include a generation of skilled and innovative individuals who drive economic and technological progress.

Equitable Education Systems: Improved access to quality education and a focus on equity could lead to long-term improvements in educational outcomes and opportunities for all students.

Healthcare Improvement:

Enhanced Health Outcomes: Gates' emphasis on healthcare innovation could lead to long-term improvements in health outcomes and the efficiency of the healthcare system. The impact might include better access to care, reduced costs, and advancements in medical technology.

Health Equity: Efforts to expand access to affordable healthcare could result in long-term progress in addressing health disparities and ensuring that all individuals receive the care they need.

Environmental Sustainability:

Climate Action Legacy: Gates' commitment to addressing climate change could have a lasting impact on environmental policies and practices. The long-term effect might include significant progress in reducing greenhouse gas emissions and promoting sustainability.

Global Environmental Leadership: By leading on climate issues, Gates could inspire other nations to take action and collaborate on global environmental initiatives. The long-term impact might include a stronger global commitment to environmental protection.

Global Development and Diplomacy:

Enhanced Global Cooperation: Gates' approach to global engagement could lead to strengthened international alliances and increased cooperation on global challenges. The long-term impact might include more effective global responses to issues such as health crises and economic development.

Continued Development Support: Ongoing support for international development efforts could result in long-term improvements in health, education, and economic opportunities in developing countries.

Ethical Governance:

Restoring Trust in Government: Gates' emphasis on ethical leadership and transparency could contribute to restoring public trust in government institutions. The long-term impact might include a more accountable and trusted government.

The legacy of Bill Gates as president would be characterized by his commitment to technological innovation, economic growth, education reform, healthcare advancement, climate action, and global leadership. His presidency has the potential to leave a lasting impact on both the United States and the world, shaping the future through transformative policies and a forward-thinking approach. Gates' leadership could result in significant advancements in technology, improvements in education and healthcare, progress in addressing climate change, and strengthened global cooperation. His legacy would likely be defined by his contributions to creating a more equitable, innovative, and sustainable future for all.

Chapter 23: Final Thoughts

Recap of Key Points

As we conclude our exploration of why Bill Gates could be a compelling presidential candidate for the United States in 2028, it's important to recap the key points that highlight his potential as a transformative leader. Gates' candidacy presents a unique opportunity to address pressing national and global challenges through a blend of technological expertise, philanthropic commitment, and visionary leadership. Here's a summary of the key points discussed throughout the book:

Background and Motivation:

Accomplishments: Gates is renowned for co-founding Microsoft and pioneering advancements in personal computing. His achievements in technology, combined with his philanthropic efforts, underscore his capability to lead and innovate.

Presidential Aspirations: Gates' interest in running for president stems from his desire to tackle complex global and domestic issues, leveraging his experience in technology and philanthropy to drive meaningful change.

Transformative Leadership:

Leadership Style: Gates' leadership is characterized by a data-driven, analytical approach combined with a commitment to ethical practices and collaboration. His presidency could bring a fresh perspective to the executive branch, emphasizing evidence-based decision-making and innovative solutions.

Vision for America:

Future Focus: Gates envisions an America that excels in technological innovation, economic growth, education reform, and global leadership. His plans include investing in emerging technologies, improving education systems, and addressing climate change.

The Microsoft Era:

Lessons Learned: Gates' experience in founding and growing Microsoft has equipped him with valuable insights into building successful enterprises, managing complex projects, and navigating global markets.

Philanthropic Initiatives:

Global Impact: Through the Bill & Melinda Gates Foundation, Gates has made significant contributions to global health, education, and poverty alleviation. His philanthropic work demonstrates his commitment to addressing critical issues and improving lives worldwide.

Global Influence:

International Perspective: Gates' extensive international work has provided him with a broad understanding of global challenges and opportunities. His global perspective could enhance U.S. foreign policy and international relations.

Economic Policy:

Economic Strategies: Gates' approach to economic policy focuses on innovation, reducing income inequality, and supporting sustainable economic growth. His presidency could bring forward-thinking strategies to address economic challenges.

Education Reform:

Educational Vision: Gates aims to modernize the education system by integrating technology, promoting STEM education, and expanding access to quality education. His reforms could prepare students for the demands of the future workforce.

Healthcare Innovation:

Healthcare Goals: Gates' focus on healthcare innovation includes leveraging technology to improve health outcomes and expanding access to affordable care. His presidency could drive advancements in medical technology and healthcare delivery.

Technology and Innovation:

Tech Leadership: Gates' expertise in technology would be pivotal in promoting innovation and enhancing digital infrastructure. His presidency could lead to significant progress in technology and digital transformation.

Climate Change:

Environmental Commitment: Gates' commitment to addressing climate change includes investing in clean energy and promoting sustainability. His presidency could advance environmental policies and contribute to global climate efforts.

Social Justice and Equality:

Equity Focus: Gates' stance on social justice includes promoting equality and addressing systemic disparities. His policies could foster a more inclusive and equitable society.

National Security:

Security Strategies: Gates' approach to national security emphasizes a comprehensive and strategic approach to maintaining safety and addressing emerging threats.

Integrity and Ethics:

Ethical Leadership: Gates' reputation for integrity and ethical leadership could set a high standard for governance. His presidency could emphasize transparency, accountability, and ethical practices.

Problem-Solving Skills:

Analytical Approach: Gates' problem-solving skills are characterized by a data-driven, analytical approach. His presidency could bring innovative solutions to complex national and global issues.

Collaboration and Team-Building:

Team Dynamics: Gates' ability to build and lead teams is crucial for fostering collaboration and achieving policy goals. His presidency could enhance teamwork and cooperation within the government.

Public Perception:

Building Support: Gates would need to address public perceptions and build support through effective communication and outreach. His campaign strategy could focus on showcasing his vision and leadership qualities.

Overcoming Challenges:

Addressing Obstacles: Gates might face challenges related to political opposition, public skepticism, and the complexities of governance. His ability to navigate and overcome these obstacles would be essential for his success.

Campaign Strategy:

Winning Strategy: Gates' campaign strategy would involve building a diverse coalition, crafting compelling messages, and engaging with various voter demographics. Effective outreach and messaging could be key to his electoral success.

Building a Winning Coalition:

Coalition Dynamics: Gates' ability to build a diverse and inclusive coalition is crucial for winning the presidency. His strategy would include engaging with different demographics, community leaders, and grassroots organizations.

A Vision for the Future:

Future Impact: Gates' vision for the future includes advancements in technology, economic growth, education reform, healthcare innovation, and global leadership. His presidency could shape the future through transformative policies and initiatives.

The Legacy of Bill Gates:

Long-Term Impact: Gates' presidency could leave a lasting legacy characterized by technological progress, economic inclusivity, educational advancement, healthcare improvements, and environmental sustainability. His leadership could have a profound impact on both the U.S. and the global community.

In my closing thoughts on Gates as a Presidential Candidate

As we reflect on the potential of Bill Gates as a presidential candidate, it becomes clear that his unique background and experiences offer a compelling vision for the future of America. Gates brings to the table a blend of technological expertise, philanthropic dedication, and global perspective that could drive significant positive change across multiple sectors.

His leadership could usher in a new era of innovation and progress, addressing critical issues such as economic inequality, educational reform, healthcare access, and climate change. Gates' presidency would likely be marked by a commitment to evidence-based decision-making, ethical governance, and a forward-thinking approach to solving complex challenges.

While Gates would face the inherent challenges of any presidential candidate, including navigating political dynamics and building broad support, his track record of success and dedication to impactful causes positions him as a transformative leader with the potential to shape the future of the nation and the world.

In conclusion, Bill Gates' candidacy represents an opportunity to bring a fresh perspective and innovative solutions to the highest office in the land. His vision for America in 2028 and beyond offers the promise of progress, inclusivity, and global leadership. As voters consider the future of the country, Gates' candidacy presents a unique and compelling choice for those who seek a president capable of driving meaningful change and addressing the challenges of the 21st century.

See You in 2028

Made in United States
Orlando, FL
08 May 2025

61141697R00046